Praise for *How I Shed My Skin*

"Simply put, a brilliant book . . . Achingly moving and intimately honest, and it does more to explain the South than anything I've read in a long, long time."

—Josephine Humphreys, author of *Nowhere Else on Earth*

"Excellent . . . layer by layer, young Grimsley sheds his deepest beliefs, prime among them that white skin bestows superiority . . . a must-read book." —*The Charlotte Observer*

"The boy in this narrative is becoming a man in a time of enormous change, and his point of view is like a razor cutting through a callus. Painful and healing. Forthright and enormously engaging. This is a book to collect and share and treasure." —Dorothy Allison, author of *Bastard Out of Carolina*

"In a world that continues to struggle with race relations, *How I Shed My Skin* is a stunning beacon of hope."

—*Shelf Awareness for Readers*

"In this sensitive memoir, Grimsley probes the past to discover what and how he learned about race, equality and democracy 'from the good white people' in his family and community."

—*Kirkus Reviews*

"Beautiful and brilliant . . . *How I Shed My Skin* does more to explore the racially inspired shootings and hate crimes of our present time than anything I have read."

—*The Washington Missourian*

"Once again, as *How I Shed My Skin* so poignantly proves, it may fall to the next generation of children to be the face of a better future." —*The Atlanta Journal-Constitution*

"Looking back some 40 years later, acclaimed writer Grimsley offers a beautifully written coming-of-age recollection from the era of racial desegregation." —*Booklist*, starred review

"Like Randall Kenan, [Grimsley] catches the weird ethos of a generation caught with one foot in *Gone with the Wind* or *To Kill a Mockingbird* and another in the world of *Star Trek* and Motown . . . *How I Shed My Skin* reminds us how far we've come in 40 years, and how far we didn't go."
—*Wilmington Star News*

"Grimsley's book illuminates a very large theme—the shadow old evil casts upon the young . . . Here, he renders history not on the grand, sociological scale where it is usually written, but on the very personal terms, where it is lived."
—Moira Crone, author of *The Not Yet*

"Vivid, precise, and utterly honest, *How I Shed My Skin* is a time-machine of sorts, a reminder that our past is every bit as complex as our present, and that broad cultural changes are often intimate, personal, and idiosyncratic."
—Dinty W. Moore, author of *Between Panic & Desire*

HOW I SHED MY SKIN

Also by Jim Grimsley

How I Shed My Skin

My Skin

Unlearning the Racist Lessons
of a Southern Childhood

JIM GRIMSLEY

ALGONQUIN BOOKS OF CHAPEL HILL 2016

Published by
Algonquin Books of Chapel Hill
Post Office Box 2225
Chapel Hill, North Carolina 27515-2225

a division of
Workman Publishing
225 Varick Street
New York, New York 10014

First paperback edition, Algonquin Books of Chapel Hill,
February 2016. Originally published in hardcover by
Algonquin Books of Chapel Hill, April 2015.
Printed in the United States of America.
Published simultaneously in Canada by
Thomas Allen & Son Limited.

Library of Congress Cataloging-in-Publication Data
Grimsley, Jim, [date]
How I shed my skin : unlearning the racist lessons of a Southern
childhood / by Jim Grimsley.—First edition.
    pages cm
    ISBN 978-1-61620-376-4 (HC)
    1. Segregation in education—North Carolina—Pollocksville—
History—20th century. 2. African Americans—Education—
North Carolina—Pollocksville—History—20th century. 3. Public
schools—North Carolina—Pollocksville—History—20th century.
4. Grimsley, Jim, 1955—Childhood and youth. 5. Whites—
North Carolina—Pollocksville—Biography. 6. African
Americans—North Carolina—Pollocksville—Biography. I. Title.
LC212.522.N8G75 2015
379.2'630975621—dc23   2014038150

    ISBN 978-1-61620-534-8 (PB)

10 9 8 7 6 5 4 3 2 1
First Paperback Edition

For the Jones Senior High School Class of 1973

CONTENTS

ACKNOWLEDGMENTS

IN WRITING THIS BOOK I am mindful that the real people from whom this story is drawn were my neighbors and friends for the first two decades of my life. I have changed the proper names in the story to preserve their privacy, though I have not changed place names or names that appear in the historical record—one example being the list of old family names from Jones County.

I have altered none of the incidents in the book, or if I have done so, it is the fault of fading memory. While these years of my life are distant, they remain vivid and present in my mind, in some ways more so than events that are more recent. Conviction that one's memory is correct means little, of course. But my aim is to tell a story that is largely my own, and I believe I have come close to the truth. I am tracing the ways in which the events of these years shaped my thinking about skin color and difference. The memory of that process has not faded.

While I have made this point in the narrative, it bears repeating that the conversations I have written are all reconstructions; I do not remember exact dialogue from fifty years ago. I have strong memories of what we spoke about as children and teenagers and believe I have presented faithful substitutes. In the cases where these little dramas recreate specific memories, they are likely to be close to the original. They are certainly as close as I can come.

To many people, I owe thanks for their help in this process, among them my family, who have once again allowed me to reach into our past and write about it. My editor, Charles Adams, and my former editor and present publisher, Elisabeth Scharlatt, have brought this story back into the Algonquin family, and I am deeply grateful for that. My former agent, Peter Hagan, helped me with this book in its early iterations, and my present agent, Melanie Jackson, has been an equally valuable voice in the final stages of its shaping. At the University of North Carolina at Chapel Hill, the staff of the Wilson Library's North Carolina Collection provided assistance in my research of the history of Jones County. The North Carolina Collection and Special Collections of the Joyner Library at East Carolina University helped me to understand the history of school integration in that region, and also provided me with microfiche access to the newspapers from Kinston and New Bern that helped to jog my memory about the years of demonstrations and walkouts at our high school. Margaret Bauer provided me with moral support and free housing in Greenville while I worked at the Joyner Library in the summer of 2013, a span of weeks that reminded me what the heat of eastern North Carolina can be like. Lynna Williams, Roxanne Henderson, Elisabeth Corley, and Kathie de Nobriga helped with early readings of the book. My colleagues at Emory University, and the institution itself, have provided the steady support on which I have come to rely.

I owe a great debt to the people of Jones County, both fifty years ago and today. Even then it was a community that was extraordinary for its closeness and caring, though it was, of course, full of the pettiness and imperfections that plague all human places. As a part of the writing of this book, I renewed contact with a number of old friends from high school days, and I would like to list them all. But since these are people whose names I have altered in the text, citing their real names among these acknowledgments would be inappropriate.

An early version of the first chapter appeared in Foster Dickson's anthology *Children of the Changing South* (McFarland, 2011); I am grateful for the encouragement that this provided.

While I have done a good deal of reading on various topics related to the subject of integration, there are relatively few facts in the book for which I have cited sources. In general, I have used my background reading as just that, and have limited the text to what I remember and knew at the time. One notable exception is the material concerning lynchings that I have included in the final chapter; information about these public spectacles of mob murder are drawn from Vann R. Newkirk's *Lynching in North Carolina* (McFarland, 2008).

At our worst we are creatures who tear at each other, feed on each other, abuse each other; at our best we are unspeakably sublime. My awe at the dreadful aspect of the human is unceasing even as I age and look beyond it to the awful dreadfulness of the universe into which I shall dissolve. When I was seventeen and headed to college, I was certain I already knew nearly everything I needed to know. I have told this story in order to reclaim some of the feeling I had in those days, including my optimism that the world could change for the better. Now I am old enough to know that I know almost nothing. While the world changes, it also stays the same, fixed by the past. Much is different between the races in the South of the third millennium, but the old ways remain side by side with the new.

BIAS

Freedom of Choice / Black Bitch

On a day in late August 1966, my little village woke to the fading edge of summer and the beginning of a new school year. A quiet dawn betrayed scarcely any sign of agitation within the placid houses, grouped under pecan or oak or elm trees, taking comfort in the shade even at that early hour, already touched with the beginnings of heat. On the main highway through town a single stoplight shuttered through its changes from red to yellow to green. The lone restaurant opened a bit past dawn to serve country breakfast to truckers and travelers and locals. Post-office workers arrived to sort mail, one or two storekeepers opened their doors, and the owner of the Trent Motel shuffled check-in forms at the front desk while the neon VACANCY sign glowed in the window.

Beyond main street under the ranks of trees wakened the rest of the village, black residents in the rows of houses we called

Back Streets, white residents in the houses we thought of as Pollocksville proper, the real place, the real world. Outside the town limits, scattered among the fields and forests of Jones County, farmers were already abroad in the early morning, continuing the tobacco harvest, readying the cured, golden leaves for market. A couple of miles from town, a clerk opened the local Alcoholic Beverage Control store, collapsing the iron security barrier against the walls, stepping behind his long counter, shelves of liquor bunched behind him in the small space. In North Carolina, liquor could be sold legally only in ABC stores, and ours was located outside of the village, decently separate from our homes and churches.

Down the highway, closer to the old Methodist church, Mrs. Willa Romley opened her fish market. At another busy intersection, Mr. Paul Arnett unlocked his thriving store on the route to the beaches. Across the county, school bus drivers, all of them students at the high school, swept their buses and started their engines. The first of the teachers arrived to inspect the classrooms.

I had begun my morning, too, slipping out of bed, skinny and pale, my white jockey shorts, my hairless body, all of me destined to begin sixth grade that morning. What I felt was mostly sadness that the free days of summer break were over. I dressed in stiff new clothes in the bedroom I shared with my brothers, new jeans and a short-sleeved shirt, a plaid that I liked, the starchy smell like a perfume in my nostrils. The night before I had carefully removed the tags, pins, and excess labels from my jeans and shirt, from my new socks and belt. New shoes made a bit of a squeaking sound as I stepped to the window to look out at the side yard. At eleven, I was in a brooding state, in my third year as a baptized Christian and member of the Pollocksville Baptist Church, attempting to resolve a belief in God with the world as I understood it from the novels of Robert A. Heinlein, P. L. Travers, Madeleine L'Engle, and Edgar Rice Burroughs. My life for the summer had revolved around Vacation Bible School, reruns of *Batman,* and walks to the public library to borrow more books. I had saved my allowance for trips to the local drugstore, where I purchased DC and Marvel comic books and read them while sipping a vanilla Coke. I wandered and daydreamed in a patch of woods on the other side of the old Jenkins Gas Company building, and read the Bible and prayed. A couple of times a week I talked to my best friend, Marianne.

On my mind that morning was the coming of the fall broadcast television season, now only a few days away, when shows like *The Monkees* and *Star Trek* were advertised to premiere. That was my consolation for the end of summer. I would be entering a new grade at school, and would have my first male teacher. I would also be going to school with black children for the first time.

On the phone with Marianne, I must have mentioned this last subject to her at some point, or she must have mentioned it

to me, and we shared some opinion about it. We had been talking regularly that summer, which made her practically my girlfriend, a thought that gave me a certain pleasure and a certain
discomfort. Most of the time we discussed Prince Charles of
England, Herman's Hermits, Paul Revere & the Raiders, other
pop bands whose music we heard that summer on *American
Bandstand.* She had told me about her family, her brother who
was really her half brother, her mother who had divorced her
first husband, her family that counted the King of England in
its ancestry. I told her about books I was reading and the work
I was doing in the family's vegetable garden. My family had no
famous ancestors, as far as I knew.

Somewhere in all of that, we must have mentioned the fact
that we would be going to school with black children in the fall.

I can no longer recall what it was like to be endlessly fasci-
nated with Marianne's accounts of what she had read in *Tiger
Beat,* or with speculation about the coming television season,
or the next rocket launch, or whether people could read each
other's minds if they tried really hard. What I can remember
is that these were the important issues in general, whereas the
news that our school classroom would include three colored
girls was harder to digest. We knew what it meant to like a
song or think a singer was pretty or cute. We had no idea what
it meant that this change called integration was coming. If we
spoke of it at all, it would have been to speculate about how
many black kids we would get in our sixth-grade class, or to

reassure ourselves that there would still be mostly white people in our school.

Marianne and I had been in the same class with the same children for all five years of our education, Pollocksville being so small that there were only enough white children to fill one classroom for each grade, one through eight. At the time, I thought all schools operated in this tidy way and was appalled to learn that in New Bern, close to us, there were two or three sections of first graders and they went to school in different classrooms. All my life I had lived in a community where whites and blacks were legally separated from one another. To the degree that I knew anything about this situation, I thought it was the natural shape of the world. Now, suddenly, there was a law that said any child could choose to attend either the white or the black school system.

The thought that I would have to sit next to black children had made me fearful when I first heard it. The fear came from what I had already learned about race, though if asked, I would likely have denied that I had been taught anything at all. To the degree that I understood the fear, I knew it came from a feeling that the world was rearranging itself, the shift being bigger than I could take in. I had a quiet conviction that change was unfair in some way, because I had hardly gotten to know the old world, when, suddenly, here was the new.

I felt the same fear when I saw news stories about demonstrations against the war in Vietnam, race riots in the inner cities,

and the possibility of nuclear war. The world was burning before I had even had a chance to grow up and enjoy it. A hol-
low settled into my middle at such times, and I found another
Heinlein novel, maybe *The Star Beast* or *Have Space Suit—Will
Travel,* and escaped into the future.

Exactly what had happened to bring about the new world
I was not sure. Outside of school or church, adults rarely explained history or taught about how things worked, leaving
us children to figure things out as best we could. Nobody ever
told me why blacks and whites had to go to separate schools,
use separate restrooms, and keep a distance from one another.
No one ever pointed out a black person to me and said, "You
cannot drink water out of the same glass as that person, or call
him 'sir,' or sit next to him in a public place." Yet the knowledge
of those truths had come into me in spite of the silence.

At church, Mr. Russell sometimes declared that God did not
intend for the races to mix. He owned the only restaurant in
Pollocksville, so the issue concerned him, since he had recently
been forced by law to serve colored customers. According to his
worldview, black people had their place just like white people
had theirs. They did not want to associate with us any more
than we wanted to associate with them. This was a statement
I would hear echoed in other voices at other times. At church,
Mr. Russell would not have used the word *nigger,* but in his
restaurant he would have. His was a voice I remember, and
some people in the small congregation agreed with what he

said. Others did not. So the uncomfortable subject never took the center of our discussions, which were largely concerned with choir practice, the building fund for the new church, and the fact that too many of the girls were wearing those new mini-skirts to Sunday service.

Likely at church I had heard the term "Freedom of Choice," the name of the new law that maintained separate school systems for blacks and whites while allowing for a certain degree of race-mixing. After service, having been reminded of their salvation during the preacher's sermon, adults stood in front of the sanctuary and talked a bit, especially in the warm months, which in eastern North Carolina comprised most of the year. I wandered among them sometimes and listened to their deep voices, their serious tones, watching as the men adjusted their ties and the women fondled their purses. Church was one of the rare places where I heard adults talk, and where they discussed the government, the war in Vietnam, and politics.

As I dressed for school that morning, I combed my hair carefully in the way that my mother had taught me, parted on the side, with a little flip at the front that she called a rabbit hill. My mother inspected it and approved. There were four children to get ready for school, and Mother herself also worked there, in the cafeteria, so she would be driving the few blocks. But I had decided to walk to school. We had lived in the village proper only a few months, and I was still delighted with the novelty. The town was huge to my eyes, and I felt immeasurably more important now that we lived in it. On leaving the house with my new notebook and pencil case, I listened to the starched sound of my new jeans with each step. I had rolled up the cuffs of the jeans over my new black shoes. The clothes felt like a kind of carapace, my shirt collar so stiff it poked at my neck. As soon as I was out of sight of the house, I rubbed the rabbit hill out of my hair. It had become important to me, lately, to take some control of the way I looked.

My thoughts were on the trivialities of the day, or my family's troubles, or the fact that I would see Marianne again. I was thinking about the fact that I would have Mr. Roger Vaughn as my teacher this year, when my first five teachers had all been women. In the same fashion, my conversations with my mother that morning were about what cereal I would eat for breakfast; that I should eat even if I wasn't hungry, because I would be hungry later; and that she thought I could wear my shirts to school twice before they needed to be washed. As in so many other cases, the biggest issue, the biggest change, went unspoken and unmarked. Never once did any adult give me any advice about how to treat the new black students in our school. On the rare occasions when I heard adults discuss integration, they spoke to one another in the coded, guarded manner typical of adults, presuming a knowledge I had yet to gain.

So I walked into the classroom and took a seat in a desk at the head of a row. The room was quiet, as best I can recall, more so than normal for a first day of school, with Mr. Vaughn sitting at his desk, droopy-eyed, nose covered with veins twining this way and that, tanned like leather from a summer at Bogue Sound. None of the school buses had arrived yet.

The three black girls walked into the classroom together, each holding a notebook and a purse. They had a wary air to them, faces stiff and frozen. As I recall, they were escorted into the room by the principal, Miss Julia Whitty, who introduced them to Mr. Vaughn and, in saying their names, spread the introduction to the rest of us as well. Violet, Ursula, and Rhonda. Miss Whitty was smiling, speaking in her confident voice, fingering the glasses she wore on a chain around her neck. She treated the girls as if they were simply new students who had moved to Pollocksville, though she knew as well as anyone that new students hardly ever moved to Pollocksville, and certainly not three at a time. In the way of beginnings, this was all. The girls took their seats.

One of them, Violet, sat in the desk behind mine. Ursula sat behind her, and Rhonda sat across the aisle. Violet's last name was Strahan. Both Rhonda and Ursula were named Doleman. They were sisters. I remember being mildly surprised at two sisters in the same grade of school. By that age I knew where babies came from and how long it took for them to arrive.

The girls talked to those of us sitting nearby that first day, but I have no recollection of what we said to one another. The three girls were very different from each other, and I stared at them a good bit. Violet was large, almost barrel-shaped, with very small breasts tucked up high on her ribs. She wore her hair short. I don't recall whether she straightened her hair that first day or whether she wore it natural, in the style that was called an Afro. Her skin was polished and smooth. Given the heat, she often wore sleeveless dresses, and in my recollection that is what she wore the first day of school, her arms perfectly smooth, a bit thin compared to the density of her torso. She spoke in a powerful voice, so much so that it was hard for her to whisper. She had fierce, hard eyes. Whenever she moved in her desk, it rocked against mine.

Ursula was younger in affect, with a pretty, rounded face and a softly curved body. She looked ample and plump, her movements betraying a certain shyness, her eyes gentle. She had the look of someone who could be friendly, who could be trusted. When she spoke, her voice was easy and lilting. She tugged at her dress from time to time, as if she were self-conscious about it, or as if it were too tight.

Rhonda had big brown eyes, long, straight hair, and a face that was lovely to watch. She carried herself with a liveliness, a sense of herself, that was complete, and she had an air of confidence that verged on defiance. She wore a pleated skirt and blouse that first day, or, at least, that is the way I will draw her. What she wore drew stylishness from her way of carrying herself, the fact that she knew who she was. Her pride was unshakable.

They sat among us thirty-odd white children, composed and prepared for whatever might come. The rest of us, who knew each other so well from five long years in classroom and on playground, who had grown so used to each other, who had established our social order, suddenly found our world was much different than before. We had dealt with few newcomers to our group.

A bell rang. Mr. Vaughn gave the clock over the door a bleary, yellow-eyed look. School began.

MARIANNE HAD COME to school in her mother's car, as she always did, wearing her brown hair tied behind her head with a girlish ribbon, her blouse with a sort of sailor's bib, her pale legs under a modest skirt. She had a mouth full of braces that made her talk a bit moist at times. I can't recollect where she sat that first day of school, though she, Virginia, and I would contrive to sit close to one another for most of that year.

I don't recall much in the way of conversation, though we must have chattered as we always did, not simply Marianne and me but all the rest of us. The boys snickered in the back of the room, told dirty jokes, had farting contests, and talked about their weekend at Catfish Lake. Friends in adjacent desks whispered to one another, girls sharing chewing gum, which they were not supposed to chew, sliding the gum into their mouths in secret.

Marianne and I talked about Batman, maybe, or about the

new show *Star Trek* that would premiere in a few days. She might have brought an issue of *Tiger Beat* to school that day, in which case she showed me a picture of her secret crush, the guitarist for Herman's Hermits, Derek Leckenby, who rivaled Prince Charles for her affections. I can hardly remember what I contributed to these conversations.

At my back was Violet Strahan, the black girl, sitting in the desk behind me.

I had an impulse to say something to her, to call her a name.

Of my memories of that day, this moment comes to me the most clearly. I had a feeling it would be funny to call Violet a name, and I knew I was daring enough to do it. The feeling of that thought in my head is far more vivid than any other detail of the beginning of school. I am fairly certain that this happened either on the first day of school or soon after. I knew that calling Violet a name would make the boys at the back of the room laugh. That moment inside my head rings down through the years so clearly. I was eleven years old, filled with a vague sense of purpose, and ready to do my part, though for what, I could not have said.

The moment was clear, sunny. Mr. Vaughn had left us unattended for some reason, maybe to smoke a cigarette in the teachers' lounge. Our schoolroom had fifteen-foot ceilings that made the sound of our chatter ring, and windows that nearly reached to the top of the ceiling. The windows would have been open, maybe a breeze coming through to stir the heat. I had the impulse to speak again, and I turned to Violet, and a moment of silence fell over the classroom, into which I said the words I had been planning. "You black bitch," I said, and some of the white boys looked at me and grinned. People giggled nervously.

Violet hardly even blinked. "You white cracker bitch," she said back to me, without hesitation, and cocked an eyebrow and clamped her jaw together.

I sat dumbfounded. There had been no likelihood, in my fantasy, that she could speak back. A flush came to my face.

"You didn't think I'd say that, did you?" Her voice was even louder than before, and her eyes flashed with a kind of angry light. Everybody was listening. The laughter had stopped. "Black is beautiful. I love my black skin. What do you think about that?"

"You are a black bitch," I said again, stupidly, blushing. Some of the white students continued to snicker and I could tell they thought I was really brave. But the moment did not make me feel the way I had thought it would.

"And you a white one," she said, folding her arms across her chest.

Pretty soon after that Mr. Vaughn returned. The moment came to an abrupt end. Violet said nothing further about what I called her. All the rest of the day, I could feel her gaze boring into my back.

She had reacted to my declaration in an unexpected way. When I called her that name, she was supposed to be ashamed, she was supposed to duck her head or cringe or admit that I was right, that she had no business being in our white classroom. If I had followed my thought far enough, this is what I would have found. But she took my insult as a matter of course and returned it. In her sharp eyes and fearlessness were evidence of a spirit tough as flint, a person unlike any of the milder beings around me.

She had a voice so big it pushed me back into my desk. To make such a sound come out of herself caused her no self-consciousness. I could sing loud in the choir but otherwise I spoke quietly. She was very different from me, but not in the ways I expected.

She was real. Her voice was big and it reached inside me. That moment lingered in my head for the rest of the day. It had ended abruptly. She had not told the teacher what I had said. We were two children, having an odd kind of fight. She had not tattled. Why had I called her that name? I used cuss words so rarely the other kids usually giggled when I did.

If I was superior to her, as I had always been told I was, why didn't she feel it, too?

An Awkward Fight

I had only a vague understanding of what had led me to call Violet such a name, and certainly at the time could not have described my reasons. At least in part, I had a desire to perform for the other white students, to prove something to them, perhaps that I was daring and brave. A longing to please other people often consumed me in school. My memory of the moment contains the thought that the boys at the back of the room would think I was funny; I liked the thought of making those boys laugh. None of us welcomed these newcomers that first day, and I would be the one to say so.

Part of my motivation was clearly that I wanted to assert power over Violet because she was black and I was white. While no one had spoken to me directly about what it meant to sit in a classroom with black students, I had gathered that it was against the good order of the world. If anyone had asked me before that morning what I thought about integration, a word I had heard only through adult conversation, I am not at all sure I could have formed a response. But the conflict with Violet demonstrated my training in prejudice to be rather well advanced. I was a good little racist, prepared to put her in her place.

What I had learned about the world had led me to believe I had the right to do so. But her reaction showed me clearly that this information, whatever it might be, was faulty. She had insulted me back and beaten me at the game of words. She had made me blush.

When she called me a cracker, she expected me to hear the word as an insult. Nobody had ever used that word to me before, except to describe a saltine. I had no idea what she meant.

She had behaved toward me just as any child would have, if we had started calling each other names out in the school playground under those tall pines. Recognition of this fact came to me after the moment was over, and a part of me changed. She might be black and large and loud, but in the end she was a child like me. This is, again, more articulate a statement than I would have made in the moment, but this was the fact that became plain in the aftermath. Violet was a person, more or less the same as me. This sounds such a small thing as I look back. But as the school day progressed, as I walked home through the hot streets of summer, this was the feeling that resonated through me.

I was timid about facing Violet again the next day, but she made it easy by getting right to the point. She looked at me with those scornful eyes and asked, "You going to call me any black bitch again?"

I shook my head at once and said no. She must have believed me since she let the challenge go. As the school day progressed, we talked back and forth across our desks from time to time, about something we were supposed to do in class, maybe, or about Mr. Vaughn, who was peculiar in ways that might invite an eleven-year-old's comment. I found ways to be friendly to her, my way of saying I was sorry, and she accepted them. She demanded nothing like an apology, at least at the time, and I offered nothing. But I signaled that I would not call her a name again, and that was enough for peace between us.

I remember being grateful that the moment faded so easily, helped by the fact that school moved forward and the long days of heat melted us into a community halfheartedly united by sweat, learning, and puzzlement at Mr. Vaughn. Even after so many years I can recall my own fascination at Mr. Vaughn's rich crop of nose hairs. He was the most peculiar of the teachers I would have in school, with his belt cinched at the level of his ribs, his tanned arms grizzled with twisty hair, and his nostrils of a size to swallow small fruit. His nose was traced with visible purplish veins, his eyes weak, his glasses large and owlish. When he spoke, flecks of spittle sometimes flew from his mouth.

He was old, at least as old as Miss White, the second-grade

teacher, but unlike her, he had lost some vital force that once might have enabled him to command a classroom. Our small town knew far too much about everybody, Mr. Vaughn included, and my friend Virginia, who lived within sight of his house, swore she heard his wife screaming at him sometimes in the evening, "Roger Vaughn, you need to get in here and wash these dishes!" Upon which summons he would shuffle into the kitchen meekly and do as he was told. Virginia told this story to Marianne and me, and since the new girls sat near us, they heard it, too. This left us with an image of him as hapless and uncertain.

He was one of three teachers our class had as sixth-graders, if I recall correctly, since for one hour a day Mrs. Ferguson taught us mathematics, and Mrs. Armstrong taught us science. These were not subjects in which Mr. Vaughn was strong. He was most knowledgeable in the teaching of history and of the classics; my sister still remembers the way he led her class through Homer's *The Odyssey*, and she was much fonder of him than I. In fact I cannot recall that *The Odyssey* was actually part of the official curriculum in our class. My most vivid memory of Mr. Vaughn is his struggle to explain rocketry to us, on one of the mornings when NASA was launching one of the Apollo missions. He thought that rockets flew straight up and hung motionless while the earth turned under them. I was aghast; even I knew better than that.

The teachers moved to our classroom rather than our moving

to theirs, likely because of Judah Carl Johnson, a student who was wheelchair bound. The teacher movements took place in the early morning, leaving us with Mr. Vaughn for most of the day. The women teachers were very good disciplinarians, which made Mr. Vaughn's lack in this area all the more obvious. We were also in class with him for much of the hottest part of the day, and there were times when he simply sat at his desk mopping sweat from his brow, or left us alone and went to the teachers' lounge. Whether he was in the class or not, we talked fairly freely.

With all the hours of the day to fill, some of us forgot that we were supposed to be racial strangers and talked to one another as friends. Virginia, Marianne, and I formed a circle of chatter with Rhonda and Ursula, and with Violet on occasion, and other people joined us from time to time. We were united by the fact that we were students and Mr. Vaughn was the teacher, by the tedium of the hot classroom, and outside the school by the shows we watched on television. As eleven- and twelve-year-olds, we had more in common than not.

The three girls were neither shy nor intimidated by the fact that white students outnumbered them ten to one. They were defiantly proud of themselves, and in their behavior, they made it plain that they were proof against any level of white scorn, like my calling Violet a bad name, or like the kind of sniping they received from the white boys in class.

"When George Wallace gets to be president, you won't think

you so big," said Harry Bell one morning, in response to something Violet had said.

"I ain't studying no George Wallace, he nothing but another cracker, he ain't got nothing going on."

"He'll stop all this mess," Harry said. "He'll help all y'all get back to Africa."

"Ain't nobody going back to Africa, baby, this is just as much my country as it is yours."

"We'll see."

"Yes, we will. Power to the people."

Back and forth. Taunting of some kind, on some subject, would likely have been the rule of the classroom anyway. But we spoke about skin color, about difference.

The fight likely began at one of those moments, and escalated when one side or the other poked at the boundary a bit too hard. It was an abortive altercation at best, between Harry and Violet. He was one of the boys who liked to make Violet mad, the son of the owner of a filling station, an only child with big blue eyes and a head of thick blond hair on a rather large head. He must have said something to Violet that day. The two of them were the ones who had the sort-of-a-fight.

Our elementary school was small, slightly more than two hundred students, eight teachers, one principal, one maintenance person, one school secretary, and three cafeteria workers. Our principal doubled as the fifth-grade teacher. Because we were so few in number, and because all our parents knew one another, the school was plagued by few discipline problems. Even the altercation between Violet and Harry was tentative and bloodless.

They had words in class, or at least this is what I imagine must have happened. The inciting incident did not register with me, though the conversation above is a good approximation. Such moments had become routine. Topics of these exchanges included assertions by the new girls that white people did not have soul, countered by giggling and scorn at the notion of soul on the part of the white boys. The girls informed us at one point that the revolution was coming, when black people would be taking over. The white boys made some weak response. The debate often moved to the topic of music. The black girls talked about black musicians like James Brown, and the white boys hooted with laughter at the notion that soul music was anything but noise.

The argument between Harry and Violet had started during one of the intervals of dispute, when Mr. Vaughn was out of the classroom, probably off once more to the teachers' lounge. Times when he was absent were opportunities for all kinds of conversation, and the exchanges between the white boys and the black girls happened in that space. But there was something different about that day's spat. Maybe Violet, who bore the brunt of the harassment, had simply taken all she could.

On the way to the playground that afternoon, Violet and Harry continued their argument. Violet commanded attention with her voice, her fierceness, and her blocklike body, small fists clenched. Soon the moment escalated, a circle formed around them, and it appeared that the two would fight. Harry appeared befuddled and flushed, and Violet glared at him with fierce eyes and battered at him with her voice. She was telling him that she was proud of her black skin. She was daring him to hit her. I recall a bit of pushing, perhaps some hands flapping.

Harry towered over her, probably outweighed her, but blushed deeply and never struck her. No fight happened, even when she stepped close to him, standing almost under his chin. Something in him refused to cross the line. Something in them both. The shouting calmed, the circle of students broke up, the boys went off to play softball in their field, and the girls and I went to jump rope.

What was said in this argument? Voices overlapped one another, confusion and challenge: go ahead and hit me, you won't do it, I dare you, ain't nobody scared of you, go ahead, call me some names, I dare you, call me some nigger—phrases on this order, the two of them circling each other, no one in the watching crowd quite sure what to do. Some of the other boys found Harry's predicament to be funny. Nothing happened that differed from any other fight between sixth-graders, or I would guess this was true, since in our quiet and usually harmonious world I had never seen a school fight at all.

While I remember the fight as being loud and lasting for three or four minutes, in our classroom afterward there were no repercussions, and I suppose Mr. Vaughn had not been near enough to be aware of it, or simply did not care.

The exchange proved that some level of human recognition was taking place in our classroom, though it was hardly universal and had no likelihood of erasing the ideas of difference to which we white people were still clinging. Harry might think black girls were inferior to him, but a part of him would not cross the line so far as to hit a girl, even when she dared him. He had always been a bit tenderhearted, an only child, spoiled and coddled, and I knew this about him in the same way that I knew too much about all my classmates, because there were so few of us. The fact that Harry found this limit in himself, though— that he would not have a physical fight with Violet—did not mean that he would ever accept her as his equal. Most of us in class, perhaps all of us, were like him in this regard. Our prejudice might find its boundaries, but it would refuse to vanish.

Tiger Beat, Teen, Ebony, and Jet

My friendship with Marianne peaked during that
year, and most people who observed us likely
thought we were caught up in a childhood romance, since we
were constantly in one another's company, talking at school all
day and on the phone in the evenings. She was the daughter of
a local farming family, and lived a couple miles outside town, a
circumstance that left her isolated and, I expect, a little lonely.
Her mother was one of the few divorcees around, with a reputation as a snob, though were that true, it would hardly have been
unusual in Jones County, where there was a good deal of pride
in ancestry. The Howard family was an old one, and Marianne
told me on more than one occasion that her family was related
to the royal family in England, distantly at least. In this she was
repeating her mother's claim.

She was a good person, with little or no snobbishness in

her own conduct, and she adopted me as a friend before I was aware of her fully, in fourth grade I think. One Christmas her mother called mine to ask that I be allowed to come to visit that day, to play with Marianne. Her mother came to pick me up in the family's car, and we spent a peaceful day at her house. She showed me her Santa Claus gifts, played the piano for me, and we talked so much that I was nearly intoxicated.

Because I was a sissy from an early age, with a slightly effeminate way of speaking and moving, my friendship with Marianne helped to ease my years in elementary school. People had started to move beyond calling me a sissy to hint that I might be something worse. Marianne wore braces, dressed oddly, and was a bit too pretentious to get along well with the other girls. We were both misfits in our way and were drawn to each other because of that. The fact that I was close to her likely helped to normalize me in the eyes of the other people in class. This was a benefit to which I was blind, and it was certainly not planned. But the effect was there.

At the time what mattered was that she had chosen me as a special friend. My family was very poor and not at all the equal of hers in social terms, though poverty was not the whole measure of a family's status in the community by any means. I felt the difference between our circumstances keenly when I visited her house, which was built of brick, with an actual dining room, much nicer than any of the houses where my family lived over the years. But that hardly mattered to Marianne.

She had introduced me to music groups like Herman's Hermits and Paul Revere & the Raiders, and to teen magazines with glossy full-page pictures of television and pop music stars. We poured over these in school. We talked about the television shows we watched, especially *American Bandstand* and *The Monkees,* and in sixth grade, during one long day in Mr. Vaughn's class, we both practiced telepathy. She read my mind and I read hers. No matter what the outcome, when she guessed my thought, I swore she had it exactly, and she did the same for me.

When I developed an obsession with Batman and Robin on the television series, and when in the sixth grade I grew a gigantic crush on Davy Jones of the Monkees, Marianne never questioned my feelings or viewed them as abnormal. As the year developed, our telepathy game grew in scope to the point that she claimed to be in mental contact with members of Herman's Hermits and I did the same for Davy Jones. Whispering from desk to desk, we shared stories of what we were learning through our mind-reading efforts.

The fact that I felt a romantic attraction to men at that age never concerned Marianne, and I accepted it myself without much understanding of what it might mean. Davy Jones was far from the first crush I had on a handsome celebrity; I had daydreamed about courting Little Joe Cartwright for a long time, living with him on the Ponderosa, my body mysteriously changed into that of a slim girl, blonde, dressed in a poodle skirt. As I aged I no longer transformed myself into a girl in the narrative; I became instead the adopted son of Davy Jones, and later of William Shatner.

Marianne never questioned the fact that we were both in love with male celebrities, and I assumed from this acceptance that she thought of me as a friend more than as a romance. I had an inkling that my preference for males was not normal, and so kept it hidden from most other people, though Rhonda also became aware of it when we began to share magazines and speak in breathy voices about Davy Jones's blue eyes.

Marianne was not the only one to supply magazines to the class. One day Rhonda brought an issue of *Ebony* magazine, and as she leafed through its *Life*-sized pages, I stared over her shoulder in some confusion. The issue in question would have been from 1966, most likely fall or winter. Perhaps what I saw over her shoulder was the September issue of the magazine, Bill Cosby and his family, his wife with her hair swept to the side in one of the iconic sixties hairdos, Mr. Cosby's hair natural, a short Afro, and their plump-faced son raising his hand to the camera. Printed on Mrs. Cosby's shoulder were the words, "Life with TV Award Winner Bill Cosby." Also on the cover was a headline that read, "Stokely Carmichael: Architect of BLACK POWER," and another, "Australia: Its White Policy And the Negro By Era Bell Thompson."

Rhonda was reading the magazine between lessons, or maybe during one of the many intervals when Mr. Vaughn lost control of our classroom and sat at his desk to consider his plight. She flipped pages idly, and I glimpsed the pictures inside. So many black people in suits, in nice clothes, smiling at the camera. I stared and stared. I had never seen black people depicted in this way before, as if they were just like white people, as if there was no social or racial difference. In my tiny world, I had been taught to concentrate on the differences, and to view them as inferior, and my limited exposure to the new girls in school had so far made only the slightest dent in my attitudes. Black people were like Miss Ruthie who lived behind my house, worn and stooped, almost weathered to blankness. They were never so smoothly urbane as these people in Rhonda's magazine. I was simply amazed.

The cover of *Ebony* was designed to resemble *Look* or *Life*, the defining photojournalism publications of the time. *Ebony*'s logo was similar in design, and there was a full-page color photograph on the cover. The paper looked to have the same gloss. All in all, this was a slick piece of work, but I was amazed. I had never dreamed that black people had their own magazines.

Pollocksville's one drugstore featured a stand of magazines and comic books, and I had become familiar with Superman, Batman, the Flash, the Fantasic Four, Captain America, Spiderman, and Dr. Strange during my visits to this shrine of publications. I had also glimpsed *Time, Life, Newsweek,* and *Look,* official adult magazines for news. I walked to the drugstore whenever I had a couple of quarters to spend. *Ebony* was nowhere to be found on those shelves, and black people were absent from the magazines and comic books I saw there. Superheroes, like lawyers, doctors, senators, governors, presidents, were white.

Nor did these professional, citified black people appear on television, with the exception of Bill Cosby in *I Spy* and, with the coming of the new television season, Nichelle Nichols in *Star Trek*. I never knew much about *I Spy*. I devoured *Star Trek*, however, starting in September of the year our school was placed under the Freedom of Choice program, and I watched Uhura, the black communications officer, with fascination. Unlike the images in *Ebony*, Uhura occupied a role that had no parallel in my world, and since I had no prejudice as to what a starship lieutenant should look like in five hundred years or so, she was fine with me. Watching her place the silver earpiece of the sub-space communicator to her ear, I accepted the picture without any resistance. She was simply part of the crew, an equal with the others. I could accept this equality when presented in these terms, as something from the future.

But when I looked at the pages of *Ebony*, I could only see the black skin, and was amazed at the fact that these were Negroes appearing in advertisements, sitting at desks, sipping cocktails, wearing fine clothes, laughing in restaurants, discussing important issues. Black people had created a world within my world, and all the categories of my world were repeated there. (It had to be "my world," you see, and their world had to be contained in mine.)

Another magazine Rhonda and Ursula brought to school was *Jet,* containing articles like, "How Dispute About Making Eve Black Almost Scuttled Bible Movie," and showcasing pretty women like "Peggy Fino, Chic model," both featured on the cover of October 27, 1966. The look of *Jet* gave me a different feeling than *Ebony,* as if I were gaining access to information that was not meant for me. Given its smaller format, it resembled *Guideposts,* the Baptist prayer magazine my mother picked up at church, but it featured pretty women on the cover and so had a bit of a lewd feeling. Mine was a world of Baptist morality, in which dancing and drinking were forbidden and women who graced the covers of magazines with their glamour were most likely bad candidates to be witnesses for Christ. The three black girls at school shared *Jet* as if it were private, passing it from one to the other, adding to my suspicion that it was a magazine I ought not to read.

So I learned about the pop culture world and its boy bands with Marianne, and became acquainted with the Black Power movement through Rhonda and her friends. They read articles in the pages of *Ebony* and *Jet* and discussed them quietly. Maybe it comforted them to bring these pictures into that hostile white enclave. From their discussions of the words of Stokely Carmichael I learned about the chant "power to the people," about what it meant to stand with one fist raised, and about the revolution that was to come, when black people would take arms and fight to overthrow white people once and for all.

When black people rose up to kill white people, there would be a list of those who would be spared. Rhonda said she thought she might put me on the list, one day when I was listening to their discussion, and Ursula agreed. By then we had become friends, or at least this was true from my side of the equation. Even Violet spoke to me with some freedom, though we had never warmed to each other. Since I had called her a bad name, albeit many weeks earlier, I had no idea how she felt about putting me on the list of those spared by the revolution, a time when most white people would die, or so the girls claimed. I was flattered that Rhonda and Ursula might want to save me. I hoped they might put Marianne on the list, too.

Information of this kind, that black people had their own magazines and could create their own world independent of white people, that black people discussed a revolution in which they gained power, added further to the changes in my ideas about reality. The weeks of school wore on, and the presence of the girls inspired acceptance in some of the white students, anger and quiet resentment in others. In this we children echoed the world of our parents. We had been taught to look for inequality in the relationship of blacks to whites, but, faced with the facts, this was becoming hard to understand.

We shared the issues of *Tiger Beat,* but never *Ebony* or *Jet.* Rhonda and I shared a crush on Davy Jones, but I stopped short of liking any of the black pop stars in the magazines, mainly out of fear. I do not recall even having asked to look at one of the *Ebony* issues, though I remember staring at the open pages whenever she brought an issue to school.

Nevertheless these images began to change me. So did the fact that a kind of desegregation was in progress all around me, on television, in the news, in the pages of mostly white magazines, and in my schoolroom. The shell of the all-white world had cracked, and color had begun to spill throughout.

I was supposed to be the member of the superior race, but my parents did not subscribe to *Look* or *Life,* or watch the news regularly, or discuss current events, or do any of the things that I imagine went on in Rhonda and Ursula's house. I had no idea what the Civil Rights Act was, or what Jim Crow was, and I had only a vague idea of what the Black Power movement meant, or why people were becoming angry at the fact of the war in Vietnam. Perhaps the black girls had no real understanding of such forces either, but at the very least they read magazines in which these ideas were discussed. They had some idea of what was going on in the world outside Jones County. I on the other hand had little or none, unless it counts that I knew Davy Jones's life story, or could give all three middle names of the lead singer for Herman's Hermits.

By then there was a group of us sitting in adjacent desks who felt an eleven-year-old's version of friendship, or at least of cordiality, toward one another, and this included Rhonda and Ursula, and Violet to a lesser degree. Most of the white girls held themselves aloof from any conversation involving the black girls, but there were a handful who, like me, apparently felt no barrier between us.

An optimist might have seen this shift as evidence that integration was beginning to work, that the girls were being assimilated into our class, but this would have been the wrong assessment. Our friendly relations were, if anything, an adaptation of courtesy. Our school was a microcosm of our sparsely populated county. Our community saw itself as a place that had no truck with fights, or with openly expressed hatred, and no room for public displays of anything beyond piety and frugality. Far more important than any idea of segregation was the imperative to be good children and behave in school. The order to behave never required any modifier.

Something was changing in me, though, and the change was real. Quietly, one day at a time, I was losing my sense that black people were different from me in the ways I had been taught. Faced with Rhonda, Ursula, and Violet, I saw them as being like me. Certainly I saw differences, especially with Rhonda and Ursula, who lived in a nicer house than mine, who read magazines, who dressed in nice clothes. The differences were not what I had been led to expect, though, and they did not add up to superiority for me or for my skin color. The issues of *Ebony* taught me this lesson in pictures. Black people looked and acted exactly the same as white people in all the ways that were important. I was too young to articulate this change in my thinking, but it expressed itself in a much more tangible way, as a shift in what I saw, how I listened, and what I felt. The machinery of my brain was receiving new information and had begun to adapt.

Included in that machinery was my own secret, that I had something inside me that drew me to handsome boys rather than to pretty girls. Still I saw no connection between that and the other layers of difference that crumbled inside me as I watched the three new girls in our class. I had no words for these ideas, not yet.

Black and Proud

One morning the three girls rose from their desks to dance to the tune of the James Brown song, "Black and Proud." Violet sang the chorus, "Say it loud, I'm black and I'm proud," and they moved their bodies to the rhythm she set. I stared and felt the movement in my bones.

Their performance was impromptu, rising out of some moment of taunting and baiting across the classroom, our teacher out of the room, the classroom dividing as it often did between the mouthiest of the white boys and the black girls. Whatever instigated the dancing is lost to my memory, but it had to be some remark related to Black Power, to the coming revolution, or to the idea that slavery times were over and done. Someone made a remark that implied the girls were ashamed of their skin color, and they rose from their desks to perform the chorus of the song.

They danced in unison, the same moves, the same grace, without so much as a signal to show that they were coordinating with one another. Had they rehearsed the moment they could not have carried it off more completely. I, who had never danced any step more complicated than the Twist, was captivated and frightened in the same moment. These girls shared this dance, these lyrics, this feeling of pride. They shared this movement with each other. Such a moment had no parallel in my world, in which Baptists like me were supposed to avoid dancing at all costs. Excessive hip movements were known to be the work of the devil.

I can still see them standing beside their battered old desks, framed against those tall windows, their fluid bodies silhouetted against the pines outside.

There was a difference between the races, all right, or at least the trio told us so. White people had no soul and could not move. Black people had soul. The evidence was the way their bodies flowed when they danced, the way James Brown's body gyrated and shook, feeling every emotion of the motion, when he sang this anthem. He was black, he was proud, he could dance. We were white, we were uncertain, and we hardly dared to move.

The idea of soul would punctuate the next decade, and its importance was clear from the first time I heard the term. It was meant to provoke envy, to advertise the fact that black people possessed a spirit of life that white people did not, and to connect those who possessed it in an extended family of soul brothers and soul sisters. Anyone could share in its benefits—anyone could listen to soul music or visit a soul food restaurant—but not everyone could possess any amount of soul. The gatekeepers of soul were black people. They decided who had it and who did not.

The soul movement crossed the borders of race far more effectively than the Black Power movement in that many white teenagers found soul music and soul singers irresistible, and many of them coveted the idea of soul from afar. My white friends, when they learned of Black Power, had no idea what it meant and were largely frightened by the idea. The idea of soul, however, as embodied in crossover music from Motown, entered white culture from many directions, even in my closely proscribed world.

In that first moment in which I witnessed the Black Power dance of the three girls in my classroom, I could feel the impact in myself. Black Power was what these girls possessed and used. They knew us so much better than we knew them. They understood that standing and dancing was not part of us, that their pride in their black skin would mock us, that their ability to move and speak in these rhythms, unified without effort, would cow us into confusion. They understood the weakness of whiteness in these terms.

Furthermore, this strength of soul gave them the courage to confront us, here in our school room, a small pond of whiteness into which they had dropped themselves, uninvited, to make the point that our days of keeping them in their place were over. This was the message of those first weeks of Freedom of Choice, of tepid and partial desegregation. Even admitting three black girls into our midst had changed our world altogether.

The notion of white unity was mocked, though none of us could have said this in words. We had no unity. We were not, in fact, one white people united for any purpose. We were listless and silent in the face of the dance, in the joy these girls felt in expressing themselves. They were free. We were left to wonder what we were.

No one had taught me to be proud of my skin color. Perhaps that feeling was supposed to be inherent in the message of white superiority, or perhaps there never was any such creature as white pride. In that moment when the black girls danced, I felt only wonder and a touch of envy, and had absolutely no sense of solidarity with the white children around me, the ones with whom I had sat in these same classrooms for the previous five years. I had no desire to remain a sullen, motionless body in a desk. What I wanted was to learn to dance and to find out that I, too, had soul.

The Sign on the Wheelchair

B y seventh grade, Marianne and I had developed our fantasy about telepathy with our favorite pop stars into a whole world system, including reincarnation, a communal mind, demons of the flame, and the beginnings of a fantasy history, parts of which I would change and employ in my own writings many years later. She had developed mind-to-mind contact with John Lennon, along with her original link to members of Herman's Hermits. I remained faithful to Davy Jones, though I would be heartbroken, near the end of the school term, to learn that *The Monkees* television show would end at Season Two. I had also elaborated a long fantasy about being orphaned and adopted by William Shatner, or more precisely by the character he played on *Star Trek,* Captain James T. Kirk.

Marianne's mental link with John Lennon was a matter of some controversy between us, since, a few years earlier, he had made his infamous statement that the Beatles were more popular than Christ. As a young Baptist I was obliged to be shocked and appalled by the statement, and had dutifully frowned on the Beatles ever since. Marianne, being an Episcopalian, took a more lofty view. I had only a vague idea what was involved in her church, and wondered whether she was actually a Catholic, a religion that was akin to devil worship, according to my mother.

Our seventh-grade classroom was the same room we had used for sixth grade, due to the fact that Judah Carl Johnson was still one of our classmates and there was no wheelchair access for the second floor. Judah Carl was one of those Southern sons who was always known by both his given names, and he had been confined to a wheelchair all his life. He wore heavy black glasses on his small, white face, and sat with his elbows sprawled on the chair and his knees looking sharp and useless. He spoke as if he could not quite draw breath. Each morning he was rolled into the back of the room by his mother, and joined in the class by his sister Pat, who had been part of our cohort all along. The Johnsons were a large family living in a tiny house, their front yard cluttered with old cars and appliances, sitting close to the road called 10 Mile Fork. There were a lot of Johnson children, Judah Carl being the oldest. He had been in my sister's class, one year ahead of me, but failed that grade. Because of him we had a ramp leading up the steps on one side of the building, and the principal had shifted our classrooms so that the seventh grade now met on the first floor of the building. We had all looked forward to being upstairs, the domain of the older kids.

Judah Carl was an angry, unmotivated student, and most of us in class were afraid of him, partly because of his handicap, and partly because he was older and a stranger to our group. He kept to himself, rarely spoke in class, adjusted his glasses from time to time, and doodled in his notebook. Teachers rarely called on him for much in the way of class participation. When he talked, his voice was reedy, bespeaking the effort with which he produced it, his lungs weak. Exactly what was wrong with him I never knew. I would be ashamed today to feel so little empathy for one so embattled, but I was a merciless twelve-year-old, caught up in my own head, and I did not like him for the simple reason that I considered him to be an intruder. It was wrong for him to be in the same class with his sister. He was one of the older kids and he should not have failed a grade. There was no logic to my dislike.

During that year, Freedom of Choice was still in force and Jones County still operated two school systems, one for black students and one for white. Violet had returned to the black school, J. W. Willie Elementary, for her seventh-grade term, but Rhonda and Ursula remained in the white school, in my class.

That our school was white, intended for white children and

white teachers, remained fixed in my mind even after a year in the classroom with the black girls, and I suspect the same was true in the minds of my classmates. I had made friends with two children, but this did not change me in terms of my interior, or in terms of my training, after only one year. If I had been asked to describe what was going on in my school, I would have said that the black girls had decided to come to the white school because it was better than their old school, or something similar. I would have fallen back on the old assumption that black people really wanted to be white and that this desire was the driver of Freedom of Choice and integration. My state of enlightenment was not advanced.

But by seventh grade the world had started to impinge on my consciousness, as slowly I learned of the riots that were sweeping the country, one black ghetto after another going up in smoke. I had an inkling of poverty as a national problem now, thanks to the Great Society of President Johnson, and I heard about something called discrimination when I listened to the news. Discrimination was something that white people did to black people to keep them in a subordinate place. An example of discrimination was using a word like *nigger.*

Furthermore, the country was fighting a war in Vietnam, and had been doing so for some time, and this event became more and more vivid as the next year passed. This was a war that had suddenly surrounded us all like a fog, coming from all sides, without a beginning or an end. I heard that we were in the war before I ever heard about Vietnam or what it had to do with my friends or me. One of my cousins died in the war that year. He was much older than I, and I never knew him, but I could see the impact of his death on my father and mother.

Our seventh-grade teacher was Mrs. Ferguson, the same person who had taught us math the year before, a woman who was smart and fierce, sharp-tongued when crossed or when making a point, contemptuous of ignorance, demanding of discipline. She was the school's best teacher of mathematics, and liked precision in speech and thought. She was a world away from Mr. Vaughn's slack posture and liver spots, his inability to draw respect and lack of talent for keeping order. His classroom had been a muddled affair in which little really mattered other than that we show up and sit in our desks without wrestling or hurling one another through the windows. Under Mrs. Ferguson, we learned.

The fact that I now considered Rhonda and Ursula to be friends, that we talked, sat near each other, studied in class together, and discussed our favorite television shows and music, meant that I had learned to accept our day-to-day association. I had grown in some ways, but I had yet to examine my comfortable world. I never imagined what this classroom was like for them, sitting there among us, knowing, far better than I did, who was friendly to them and who was not. Knowing that many of us were thinking of them as unwelcome niggers, even if we were not allowed to say so. I had no inkling yet of the world in which Rhonda and Ursula really lived. What I knew of black people in Jones County was still limited to these two girls and the inside of this classroom. Behind them was the mystery of their parents, their families, the other people they knew, their church, their kitchens, their suppers, breakfasts, Sunday dinners.

Judah Carl personified hatred in some ways, and suffering in others. He drew the Confederate Stars and Bars on his notebook. This might have endeared him to many of the kids in school, since there was often a good deal of talk about the South rising again in our classroom. But Judah Carl was withdrawn into his own world, speaking little to anyone, making no attempt toward friendship. He appeared to have little relationship to his siblings, and Pam, his sister, who had been my classmate since first grade, hardly spoke to him.

One day he came to school with a piece of cardboard in the side of his wheelchair with the words I HATE NIGGERS scrawled in dark marker.

This is an incident that I remember far too dimly, a fact that speaks to the speed with which Mrs. Ferguson eliminated the problem. I do not know whether Rhonda or Ursula ever saw the sign or heard of it, thought I expect they did. Judah Carl was wheeled to the principal's office very quickly, almost directly after I read the sign myself. Few members of the class knew why Mrs. Ferguson took him out of class, and those who did barely had time to snicker.

His posture as Mrs. Ferguson wheeled him away was unchanged. Whatever birth defect he suffered from had caused his body to atrophy from disuse, so that he appeared sunken into himself, his hands moving almost of their own accord. He adjusted his black-framed glasses and settled deeper into the chair.

When he returned, his face was flushed red, his expression sullen, and the sign was nowhere to be seen.

The fact of Judah Carl's open hatred remained with us in the classroom through that day. He had expressed something that others felt, too, and the words echoed even when the sign was gone.

Mrs. Ferguson had a grim and unhappy face. She looked as if she did not exactly know what to do. This was a fearful revelation, that she could find herself without a clear direction, she who was always so certain and sure. She had acted to stifle this moment of ugly expression to preserve the order of the classroom and to maintain the important layer of courtesy with which Southern transactions were tinted. I am certain she had real concern for Rhonda and Ursula and their feelings in this moment. But even worse was the breach of good order that would have resulted from a confrontation between the girls and Judah Carl—and, by implication, with the rest of us. This was what she was at pains to prevent.

Polite Southerners did not use the word *nigger;* there was no one better mannered than Mrs. Ferguson, and she was shocked at the attempt, just as she would have been if Judah Carl had printed I HATE BITCHES on his sign.

Looking backward, what I see is that my classroom, placid on the surface, was in fact laced with hatred. Judah Carl attempted to express his feelings openly and so committed a breach of etiquette for which he was reprimanded. But the school made no effort beyond the maintenance of discipline and politeness to educate us about our need to accept one another. The world of white adults remained mostly mum on the issue of integration, leaving us, their children, to puzzle out the meaning of these changes on our own. We were too young for the task, and most of us simply tried to figure out what the adults wanted us to think, taking in their ideas, imitating their hatreds and prejudices.

After that day, Judah Carl sank back into his wheelchair, remote and unhappy, less inclined than ever to do his homework, to speak in class, to smile. Steps had been taken to change his behavior. No one had the power to change what he thought.

The Kiss

I had grown so used to Rhonda and Ursula by seventh grade that they were a comfortable part of my day, and since I was always good at making friends with girls, we spent a lot of the school day talking across the aisles.

"You read books all the time," Rhonda said to me, as I was closing the cover of *Have Space Suit—Will Travel,* a Robert Heinlein novel I had bought for a dime at the library book sale.

"You like that space stuff," Ursula said. "Like that *Star Trek.*"

"I don't like anything like that," Rhonda said.

"My mom won't let me stay up that late," Marianne interjected, showing her braces, her mouth a maze of metal and rubber bands. "But I like Mr. Spock."

"How do you know you like him if you don't look at the show?" Rhonda asked.

"He has pointy ears. I like pointy ears."

"You crazy," Ursula said, shifting a bit in her seat, pulling down her skirt with a tug, the hem tight over her thighs.

"You look at *Lost in Space*? That show is so stupid." Rhonda had a certainty about herself, a way of holding her face to the light, a beauty. "That robot is so dumb, talking about 'Danger, Will Robinson.'"

"I think that robot is silly," Marianne said. "It's not even real, it's just a man in a can."

"You like Will Robinson?" Ursula asked me. "He has freckles like you."

Or another day, Ursula said, with a peculiar fluid motion of the neck, "Power to the people, right on."

"What?" I asked.

"That means the revolution is coming," she said. "When the Black Panthers taking over."

"Oh," I said, with only a vague idea of what a Black Panther was.

"I like it when James Brown sings that," Rhonda added, shifting in her seat, the wood creaking a bit. Our desks bore the engravings of decades of students on the wooden work surfaces, and many of the seats made a good deal of noise at the least movement.

"Who is James Brown?" Marianne asked. "Is he like a singer?"

"He has soul," Ursula said. "He makes soul music."

"What's soul?"

"Soul is when you know how to move." She did a bit of a

shimmy in the desk to demonstrate the kind of moving she meant.

"Do white people have soul?" Marianne asked.

"Sometimes," Rhonda said. "But most of y'all don't have any."

When *Rowan & Martin's Laugh-In* premiered on television, we immediately seized on the catchphrases from the show, parroting them like everyone else did. We chanted "Sock it to me sock it to me sock it to me" as fast as we could, like Judy Carne, and on occasion we threatened to sock it to one another, to boot. When Mrs. Ferguson bustled into the room, all energy and focus, one of us might whisper, "Here come the Judge, y'all," and the rest would giggle into our hands. We had to be careful of that kind of behavior, however. Mrs. Ferguson appeared to know everything that went on in her classroom, and she had a sharp tongue for scolding. None of us wanted to test her.

(These moments are true, even if the conversations themselves are not quite literal. My memory is not so fine that it yields whole dialogue from such a long time past. But these were our voices, and these are the subjects we would have covered, given that we chattered about the world in these terms: what TV we watched, what phrases we remembered, what bits of news we heard, and what adults did and said.)

"All this stuff about Vietnam on the news," Ursula said.

"You might get drafted," Rhonda told me.

"No, I won't," I said. "They won't take me."

"Because you a bleeder," Ursula said. "That's right." She was using the short form of the term "free bleeder" by which my classmates understood my hemophilia. Teachers had cautioned our class, year after year, that I was not to be touched or struck for any reason, because I would then bleed to death and die. Even Rhonda and Ursula had heard the tale twice now.

"Can you have sex?" Rhonda asked in a whisper. "Because of your blood?"

Marianne giggled at the word *sex*.

I shrugged. "I think so."

"But you might bleed. Then you would die."

I had no idea what that meant, since my ideas about sex were uninformed; I had heard the process described by some of the boys in class but it sounded so awful I was certain it must happen by accident, perhaps when a man rolled on top of a woman in his sleep. What did blood have to do with sex, anyway?

Ursula said, "I bet he can do just like anybody else can."

"You don't know."

"I bet he can."

Ursula had struck me as shy at first, though on coming to know her, I understood that her temper was the more fiery, and her nature the more ardent. They bore comparison not because they were both black but because they were sisters. She had a less extravagant beauty than Rhonda, her body sturdier

and plumper, her hair short, sometimes straightened and sometimes not. Her clothes must have felt tight on her, because she
adjusted them constantly; this was an era of young women tug-
ging at defiantly short skirts. About Rhonda I always had the
sense that she was easy in herself, happy with her body. About
Ursula, I noticed the constant fidget.

Rhonda was the more outgoing; she was friendlier, readier to
talk and share. Ursula was tender and fragile, harder to know,
slower to return liking. Rhonda had an overt strength, while
Ursula's was quieter and more hidden. What Rhonda felt or
thought lay on the surface and expressed itself more easily.
Ursula kept her feelings to herself, at least the personal ones.
She had the courage to express herself about her blackness, and
her temper was quite strong and apt to flash out when she felt
wronged. Rhonda's anger ran deeper and lasted longer.

We must have heard that our country experienced the Summer of Love in 1967, but at thirteen years old I was terrified
of the word. The students in our class played boyfriend and
girlfriend games, same as any other group of children our age.
I can't much remember who was coupled with whom in the
class at that point, since the attachments were brief, consisting
of little more than hand-holding, note-passing, and maybe a
brief interlude of fondling in one of the closets at the back of
the room. I had done a bit of note-passing in the early grades,
little or no hand-holding, and no fondling at all. Marianne and

I never discussed becoming formally enthralled to one another at any point, and we certainly never held hands or passed notes.

There was something wrong with my conception of romance, and by that year I could feel it.

There was this boy in my class, named Robert.

He was older than me, having failed fifth grade, with a reputation for wildness, though in his case this added to his prestige among the rest of us, probably because he was handsome. Wildness for a seventh-grade boy had to do with some kind of exploit with liquor, or guns, or girls. In Robert's case, I never entirely knew what it meant. He was an only child, known for his physical strength. I was aware of him in some manner that was different from anyone else I knew. I had tutored him in math for a couple of days, while Mrs. Ferguson worked with the other students in the class. During the work, a closeness had come to the two of us, something that I felt inside my body as a kind of comfort when I sat next to him, heard his voice, or, later, even when I thought about him. These feelings were related to romance, but I was having them about another boy. I accepted this, but wondered what it meant.

This experience was not new, and my obsessions about young men in magazines and on television were not new, but my awareness was changing. I understood now that this kind of desire would mark me with difference. My hemophilia protected me from teasing to a degree, and explained the fact that I was a sissy in a way that would satisfy other seventh-graders.

I rested in that uncertain security for the moment. But I was coming to understand that this safety would not last.

No one had ever singled me out in that particular way, by making me the object of a crush.

The day Ursula kissed my cheek, I remember in this way: the core of the memory is the kiss. I have the feeling that we were in spring, in the freshness of afternoon, windows open in the classroom; that flash of bright afternoon light, a breeze, a feeling that we were nearer the end of the school year. Whenever I remember that day, these glimpses come with it.

I was standing at the chalkboard, having decided to sit inside through the break from classwork. This might have been our physical-education hour, which was really no more than playtime, when we were allowed outside. That day I had elected not to leave the room, as had some of the others, girls mostly. Judah Carl sat in his wheelchair staring at his notebook, or out the window. Maybe Marianne was at her desk whispering to Virginia. Mrs. Ferguson had left the room.

Maybe Ursula and I had been talking? We must have been, or she would not have felt whatever feeling carried her so quickly next to me. She kissed my cheek, made it warm, and murmured something. I remember the surprise of the moment more than anything else. After that, I remember her face, full of some delight, she having decided to cross this boundary, to kiss my cheek in public, to tell me I was sweet. This expression on her face is what I remember. The surprise came in the next moment, realizing that Ursula liked me. I had not known. Then, next, came the understanding that she was not supposed to like me that way.

Immediately shy, Ursula ran out of the room. I remember the look of her running, body leaning forward, hands held low, feet splayed a bit, a child in a flush of feeling. I could still feel the print of her lips on my skin. I was surprised and sat at my desk. I could feel the other students staring. One of them asked another, surely: "Did she just kiss him? Did they just kiss each other?"

To be kissed by a girl so unexpectedly, for the first time in my life, left me speechless and fearful, because the kiss was public, and because the girl was black. Ursula was not supposed to kiss me in this way. I knew this without asking, in the same way that I knew Robert was not supposed to kiss me, either. I had never heard anybody speak these rules out loud, but it had been built into me as if it were hardware. Now this had happened, a girl had liked me and kissed me and people had seen it, and this was exactly why integration was a bad idea, wasn't it? The fact that a black child might kiss a white child?

I told Mrs. Ferguson what had happened, not knowing what else to do or what reaction to expect. I feared what my classmates would think, but I cannot remember a single specific reaction. Ursula would not look me in the eye when she came back into the room. We passed a few hours of awkwardness,

Ursula quiet and uncomfortable, same as me. After that, the incident vanished in terms of classroom import. It remained in my head for a while longer as I wondered whether I should tell my parents or whether I should become more upset about the kiss. I decided to say nothing at home and to forget. Within a few days, Ursula and I were simply friends again, though we retained a kind of closeness afterward. I knew now that she really did like me. I felt pleased about that. Even though I knew I was not the kind of boy who would ever feel romance for a girl, I was pleased that she had feelings for me in that way. At the same time, without any contradiction, I was wondering about the implications of the action, that a black girl had kissed me. I had allowed a kind of contact that was not supposed to happen. But since it had happened, what was I supposed to feel? Anger? If a black girl was not supposed to kiss my white face, should I not be more convinced after the fact, and not less?

Would I have been as surprised and frightened if a white girl had kissed me on the cheek? If Marianne had kissed my cheek, I think I would have felt the same shock, though without any fear of a reaction from my classmates other than the usual teasing. I think I would have been more frightened if it were Marianne because of the closeness that was already between us. Would I have told the teacher? Even with the fact of witnesses, I would have waited to see whether anyone tattled. I would certainly have kept the secret from my parents.

This moment provides a snapshot that captures me with my prejudice still intact. I am certain my fear of Ursula's kiss was different from what I would have felt had she been a white girl.

But even so, the sweetness of the kiss lingered, and when the surprise faded, I liked Ursula better, because she had preferred me.

What might I have done had I been a straight boy? I have no way to answer this question at all. I can speculate that I might have liked her as a girlfriend, maybe in secret; but it is as easy to imagine that we would not have had any connection as friends at all. As a heterosexual, I would have been part of the boys' group, perhaps, ruled by the need for their approval. That might have prevented any friendship with Ursula.

What would have happened if Robert had kissed me that way? Or if, through some fantastical misjudgment, I had done the same to him? Of course, these ideas never came to me then. I did not live in a universe where such a thought was even possible.

ORIGINS

The Hierarchy of Place

I had found this bias against black skin in myself. I had known it was there but had not understood what it meant. Such a bias was only natural, or so I had learned, since black people themselves were inferior. I thought of Rhonda and Ursula as my friends, true, but, at the same time, I thought of them as black people, as something different from me. As something not as good as I was. My experience was colliding with my upbringing. Where had these ideas come from?

Looking backward, what can I see? If I was taught to discriminate between colors of skin, when did these lessons happen, and how did I come to absorb them?

The first part of the answer must come from the place itself, a tiny village in an old county in the eastern part of North Carolina. The first part of the story must come from my place in the South.

To hear the tale as it is commonly told, the Southerner is a creature of place, formed by a connection to the earth, to the soil, to the rivers and swamps and ponds. I was born in the country and grew up there. When I think of home, it is this landscape that comes to mind, that flat land east of Raleigh, two-lane roads curling around and over rivers, farmland opened on either side, a line of pines along the horizon, sometimes, though, marching right up to the road, standing alongside, tall as guardians. Loblolly and longleaf pines, dogwoods, oaks, elms, a green country, soft with grasses, ferns, blackberry tangles, moss.

Jones County was a hard place to love: poor, flat, thinly populated, with few comforts or amenities, racially divided. Even the people we called rich would have appeared poor in most places, I expect. But the country was quiet, the roads splitting and disappearing into mossy forests, the rivers and streams meandering. The people had taken on the quiet of the land and had sat on those roads and in those fields for two centuries or more, most of them. Stubborn, stingy, mean, and hard, with a goodly layer of religion and a way of feigning warmth and courtesy. These were my neighbors and friends, my schoolmates and church buddies. We knew each other by name and often by history, though my family, being outsiders, not native to the county, were not full citizens of the place. We would be interlopers, at best, until we had lived there a generation or two.

The county had always been poor, sprinkled with a few of

the very rich, who nevertheless were wealthy in field and forest and movable goods rather than in money. Family names such as Foscue, Foy, Pollock, Banks, Ipock, Howard, Bender, Duval, and Simmons dated back to the first settlements. People of many nationalities had moved into those early forests in search of land to claim for themselves. French, German, Swiss, English, and Scottish settlers had taken land at New Bern, where the Neuse and Trent Rivers came together. They spread along the two rivers, cleared a bit of land, built houses, bought slaves, killed and expelled Native Americans. The county never became populous, and never attracted much in the way of industry. For generations the same families farmed the land, hunted the forests, fished the rivers, and eyed each other with suspicion. In each generation, many of the children found greener pastures and moved away, while a few stayed behind.

Viewed from the most basic perspective, the history of the place can be summarized rather simply: People farmed, hunted, raised families, parts of which dispersed into the world, and parts of which stayed on the old land in the old place. Complications might come to Jones County from beyond its borders, but within them it kept to a simple pattern. Small settlements remained that way. Roads wound through forest, houses clustered at crossroads, river settlements grew to be villages, but at a certain point all that reached a limit. None of the villages grew very big. Most of the land remained forest. Most people made their living from the land.

The history of my little home village of Pollocksville is equally stark. Historical records, to the degree that they exist, describe a settlement that grew up where a road from New Bern crossed the Trent River. The intersection attracted boat traffic, merchants, and a few businesses in service of the surrounding plantations, huge tracts of land owned by Foys, Foscues, Pollocks, and others. One of the planters deeded land for the town that had by then grown to surround the cluster of stores, a lumber mill, boat landings, and the bridge. Its founding as a proper township followed that of its stuffier, more snobbish neighbor, Trenton, by a couple of decades, and was delayed further by a disputed rendition of the name. The proper spelling of *Pollocksville* would prove to be a curse for its residents from that time forward. All my early life, in the days of Polack jokes, I heard the same tired mispronunciation, "Polacksville," from anyone who heard where I lived.

When speaking of history, it is traditional to include in the biography of any Southern place the outline of what happened there during the Civil War. White Southerners rarely speak of the mark made on the past and on the landscape by slavery, though they are quick to highlight any ancestors who had wealth. Old records speak of a family's fortune in terms of the number of black people they owned, so often that it is clear that slaves and wealth were synonymous. Black people were the riches, and they shaped the landscape. When the war granted them ownership of themselves, and when railroads opened up transportation routes unconnected to the old rivers and roads, the wealth and vitality of early Jones County began to wane. What remained was the scar of ownership, one race over the other, unresolved and undiscussed.

During the Civil War, Jones County served as a battle-ground between Union troops stationed in New Bern and rebel troops stationed in Goldsboro, and for some two years it was laid waste. One soldier's account from the era speaks of a trip through Pollocksville when he could see only one family still in residence there. It is the romance of this war, this wasteland, that colored the past afterward, drawing a veil over the time that came before it. We spoke of the war but never of its real causes, describing our defense of a Southern way of life rather than admitting we fought to preserve human ownership of hu-man chattel. We spoke of slavery as an inevitability, an unavoid-ability, a misunderstood and historical necessity; but most of the time we did not speak of it, and certainly were taught very little about it in the years when I was young.

In the years after the war, Jones County followed the general outline of its neighbors, suffering and rebelling during Recon-struction, even lynching a sheriff described in one source as a carpetbagger. Our county provided the Senate with a sena-tor, Furnifold Simmons, during end-of-century elections that functioned as a national referendum on white supremacy. The nineteenth-century population of about four thousand swelled to about ten thousand, and stayed there. Teachers founded schools in the various communities, nearly all of them identified by race. The schools evolved as ideas about education changed, consolidating from many locations to a handful: Comfort, Maysville, Trenton, and Pollocksville. This pattern was settled by the time I enrolled in first grade; there were two schools in each village, one for black students and one for whites. In Trenton, there were two high schools, one for blacks and one for whites. The county struggled to operate two school systems side by side when in truth it could barely afford to run one.

Through all this, Jones County folk farmed the fields, growing tobacco, soy beans, corn, even a bit of rice. No one I knew grew cotton in the 1960s, due to the impact of the boll weevil, though my mother told stories about working in the cotton fields when she was a child. Men and women hunted and fished, sportsmen stalking black bear and deer while those feeding their families aimed for smaller game. In spring and summer people planted gardens and harvested tomatoes, pole beans, eggplant, yellow squash, bell peppers, okra. We attended church, organizing our social life around it. White people kept black people at a distance, confined them financially and legally, and perpetuated a worldview in which this treatment was right and proper. On occasion, ugly and savage events occurred in the neighboring counties, and in Jones County, too: crosses were burned, people were lynched. Acts of terror mixed with everyday life.

PEOPLE DID NOT often immigrate to Pollocksville, but we Grimsleys had done so. My father had taken a job on a farm called Ravenwood, a remnant of an old plantation. He had a family connection with the farmer who owned the land, and we moved into a cinderblock house there when I was six months old. What was left of Ravenwood belonged to a man named Dixon MacArthur. He was in business with a farmer named Grimes in Pitt County, with whom he provided hybrid seed corn to area farmers. My father and some of his brothers worked on Mr. Grimes's farms in Pitt and Edgecombe Counties, and later my father brought us to Jones County to work on Mr. MacArthur's end of the operation. Father worked as a foreman until the day he tried to clean off the belt of a cornpicker while it was still running. He caught his hand in the machine, which shredded his arm and nearly tore it off. Doctors in New Bern amputated the arm and buried it there somewhere. After that, my father lost his job on the farm and worked for the local bottled gas company, delivering liquid propane to farmers to cure their tobacco crops in the summer. My father's accident provided a narrative that shaped my early life, a story that people told about my family to mark us as relative strangers to Jones County who had brought our own doom with us, apparently, when we moved there.

The farming accident that cost my father his arm and his job embittered him for the rest of his days. My family moved from the somewhat respectable status accorded the foreman of a large farm to the poverty of a laborer, someone who drove a truck. As a deliverer of bottled gas and a man who could repair most appliances, my father became something of a local legend. People liked to say he could do more with one arm than most men could manage with two; in fact, they liked to say it so much I think they would probably have said it even if it were not true. That he was an alcoholic, a wife-beater, and a schizophrenic descending gradually into madness were simply additions to the color of his reputation. Most Southern men flirted with a drinking condition, if not outright alcoholism. A man's home was his castle, in the parlance of the era, and he had a duty to smack his wife a time or two if she behaved badly, as women were apt to do. Everybody had a crazy relative. This was the land of Southern gothic, after all. We were the heirs to Southern darkness.

People like my father became part of the landscape, a feature of the town, his one arm and the story of its loss a piece of the local history. The fact that we were part of a story meant that we had become attached to the place, since involvement in local stories was the proof of belonging, and the telling of them was confirmation. In this, though my family was generally accepted in Pollocksville, we were at a disadvantage. We did not know enough of the history, we could not tell the stories of the local boys who had marched off to war, or hunted the ranges of forest, or fished the rivers. We could not join in the gossip about the local families, being ignorant of who had married whom and who had wronged whom over the last several generations. We meant to put down roots in Jones County, and to a degree we did, but our roots were young and shallow compared to the other families who had been sitting on this soil, feeding from it, for a hundred or two hundred years or more.

OUR TOWN HAD no movie houses, no supermarkets, hardly a single clothing store, and only one restaurant. We had churches in abundance, and church events ruled the calendar, with nothing but high school athletics for competition. In my Baptist church, Sunday morning brought church service, Tuesday night was choir practice, and Wednesday was prayer meeting, with the occasional business meeting and the occasional revival to punctuate the seasons.

To say that our lives were quiet is not to claim that they were simple in any way. In the quiet places of the world, human nature becomes convoluted, spreads out to claim more space for its twistings, and makes knots of the Gordian variety. The countryside and its beauty sheltered much that could be described as gothic, and hid many a blemish. Old houses fell down into heaps of lumber, overgrown with weeds and vines, while next door, or in the backyard, the family parked a mobile home or built a new cinderblock house. Yards overflowed with old appliances and rusted cars. Torn screens hung from porches on a house crying for paint, unlikely to be soothed.

Old tobacco-curing barns collapsed or leaned to the side next to the metal-sheathed bulk curers that dried the tobacco much faster. The past collapsed and decayed even as the future replaced it.

One fine plantation house on the road to Trenton still stood during my childhood, and we passed it often enough that I remember it, a white-columned structure down a long lane lined with oaks. I would learn much later that the house had originally been quite modest, a one-story frame farmhouse, but the owners had long ago, likely long after the Civil War, raised it by one floor and added a neoclassical porch. The Simmons family, who lived in the house, owned many square miles of land thereabouts, parking a private plane behind trees on one side. On the other side of the house stood a row of what were rumored to be old slave cabins, and we pointed these out to each other over and over again as we passed them. That is where the slaves lived, we would say, as if this were an important fact to remember. So it was that a ride through the country could show me something of the hierarchy in which we lived, rich and poor, black and white. Geography provided a lesson in who was high and who was low. I marveled at the thought that somebody could own and fly a plane, and there it was, behind a row of trees. But I hardly blinked at the thought that the same family had once owned slaves. I do not remember a time when this fact was new to me. It was a part of the background, something I had learned earlier than memory.

People in the county took jobs in the logging industries, at the sawmill in Pollocksville (until it burned), at the DuPont plant in Kinston, at the schools, or in county government. They delivered bottled gas or fuel oil, or sometimes ran a small business. After the accident, my father made a living first at the gas company, and later worked for himself, installing central air-conditioning and heating systems, repairing refrigerators and freezers, occasionally selling new ones. The county and surrounding areas provided work in house construction, roofing, plumbing, bricklaying, and truck driving. These employment opportunities, however, were scarce, and jobs were precious.

On Main Street of Pollocksville stood service stations, a post office, an antique store, two general stores, a small drugstore where the proprietor also wrote insurance policies, and a pool hall, the latter being the closest we came to possessing a den of iniquity. The state-owned liquor monopoly sold liquor legally from its store a couple of miles outside of town, and some of the local people built private stills and sold moonshine. A dry-goods distributor kept a small warehouse on Main Street near one of the two barber shops, the one owned by the younger barber, where town boys went to get cooler haircuts than the older barber knew how to give. There was a beauty parlor in town, opened by one of the local daughters when she graduated from cosmetology school. These businesses were owned by white people. Black businesses were rare, and I can remember only a second pool hall and a shoe-repair shop, these being

located in nearby Hatchville. This means only that I was ignorant of any black businesses nearby and not that they did not
exist.

The isolation of Jones County was a state of mind. A saying
that we repeated from time to time ran something like this:
"There is a right way to do things, and a wrong way, and a Jones
County way." That third alternative, mixed of right and wrong
no doubt, defiant of both, grew out of centuries of stubbornness, a rural life interrupted only occasionally by the events of
the greater world.

There were good people in that town, and I grew up there
with a feeling that a community surrounded me, that I was
known and recognized wherever I went. Perhaps that would
have been enough if my eyes had never opened, if the world
had never changed. There was peace and safety in that town,
and probably for most people in the county, as long as we each
knew our place and kept to it.

THE SOUTHERNER WHO feels a rich connection to a
place is mostly likely nostalgic for that place the way it used
to be. Place is history, not because the connection between the
two is inevitable, but rather because the past has become ideal-
ized, covered with the gauze of memory, softened and obscured.
The Southern dream of place is choked with longing. For the
white Southerner, the past was a better time than the present,
even though it was tragic and painful. For all this supposed

link between the Southerner and history, the obsession with the past, the South is not inhabited by students of history. People were more inclined to repeat truisms about the past than they were to read the documents and learn the facts. The Southerner is comfortable with oral history, with tales spoken from mouth to mouth, and suspicious of the rest. The Southerner is comfortable with a view of the past that is inherited without much question. Stories change in the telling, and even more in the repeating. The past is bendable and adaptable. We see in it what we will.

Place is hierarchy, above all. This sense of Southern place, and of any Southerner's given place, is entwined with that other notion of attachment to the land. The Southerner was indeed expected to know his place, not simply in a geographical or mythological sense, and to accept this place and adhere to it. The Southerner had a position in the social order: white trash, slave, merchant, overseer, paddyroller, artisan, master. This functioned as a kind of temperature, which moved up or down with one's fortunes or behavior. Knowing your place in the world and accepting it, paying respect to your betters and giving a good kick to those beneath you, these were and are part of the Southern order.

A Southerner accepted his station in life but tried to find the means to rise above it. That same Southerner accepted the station of others in life and tried with all his might to keep them in it. The Southern world spent much of its energy deciding who was entitled to advantages and who was not, and most especially who was better than whom. The social hierarchy was complicated and endless, Southern memory long and vengeful. Violations of the social order, lack of respect for one's betters and their relations, brought quick retribution along with slow and thorough revenge.

God never put us equal onto the earth. The very notion was absurd. God put us in a hierarchy, some better and many worse, and He gave us life so that we could discover who was the better and who was the worse. Southerners have never believed in equality, even when they have believed in some kind of democracy. The two ideas have never had much association with each other.

In this, I am mostly speaking of the white Southerner, though I don't doubt that black and brown Southerners share some of the same traits. The history I mean to trace here is my own white history, in which I grew up with an assigned place, one low in the Southern social order. I was raised to be a believer in the United States as a white nation, in the South as a white paradise, and in the superiority of my European-descended race over all the other races of the earth. No one ever said these words to me in such clear terms, but, nevertheless, I learned the ideas behind these beliefs. In particular, I was raised to keep black people in their place, and to see to it that they stayed there. My purpose here and now is to examine how good people perpetuated this in the raising of their children and in the living of their lives in my part of the South. Or, to be more personal, my purpose here is to examine how, as a child, I learned bias against black people from the good white people around me. For there is no one else from whom I could have taken this lesson.

The Learning

M AYBE THE INSTRUCTION began with nursery rhymes.

Nigger, nigger, black as tar
Stuck his head in a molasses jar
Jar broke, nigger choked
And went to heaven in a little rowboat

I learned this rhyme early enough that the memory of its origin escapes me, so that the doggerel appears to exist in my head from birth. The verse was useful for the clapping-hands games that I played with girls, or the jump-rope sessions in which I sometimes participated. Like that of a good pop song, the rhythm of the stanza stuck in the brain so that the words repeated themselves over and over again. I chanted this verse before I knew what a Negro was, late in the 1950s as I woke up to being, three or four years old, suddenly stuck in the world, trying to figure it out.

We played games around the tobacco farms or near the back doors of houses, our mothers visiting inside, sipping thin coffee in the kitchen, children in the dirt yard kicking aside the sweet-gum balls and saying whatever nursery rhyme or scrap of a country song we knew. We played tag or hide-and-seek or we ran with tobacco sticks between our legs, pretending they were horses and we were the Lone Ranger and other cowboys. I remembered some songs we sang, a Kitty Wells divorce song, Johnny Cash when he heard the train a'coming, a'rolling around the bend near Folsom Prison; I knew "Silver Threads and Golden Needles," and I knew the nigger rhyme.

> Eeny meeny miney moe
> Catch a nigger by the toe
> If he hollers, let him go
> Eeny meeny miney moe

This rhyme was used for selecting, often to determine who would be "it" in a game of tag or the first seeker in a game of hide-and-seek. We children chanted, pointing from one to the other on each beat of the verse, and the person on the last beat was chosen; a chorus of shrieking greeted the selection. Sometimes a person might say "rabbit" in place of "nigger," but mostly we said "nigger."

Children chanted these verses in play, mixed in with "Pop Goes the Weasel," "Little Miss Muffet," and "Ring Around the Rosey." In such a way the notion of *nigger* entered my brain and stayed, starting likely before I knew language myself, listening to the sounds of other children at play. In chanting these rhymes I was learning a word that would shape my view of the world, and my knowledge of what a nigger was would thereafter organize itself and grow.

I played with other children at Lee's Chapel United Methodist Church, in the interval between Sunday School and the main service. This took place once a week. Later, in school in my hometown of Pollocksville, playtime would become a daily routine. I played with cousins at family gatherings in Rocky Mount, where my father's family originated, or in Princeton, where my mother's people lived. The rhymes were ubiquitous and, attached to the supposed innocence of play, taught me their lessons through the medium of fun. Learning them in the shadow of the church or in the pine-shaded schoolyard, knowing their acceptance by the adults around me, meant that the word was acceptable, at least to a degree. Women who might have objected to the casual use of *nigger* as a word, on the grounds that it was not nice, nevertheless accepted it in the guise of a child's rhyme. A child might be corrected for calling someone a nigger at the wrong time or place, or using the word in a sentence in polite company, but adults might not object to the chanting of an old rhyme in the yard during a game of jump rope. The doggerel was a part of play.

Adults in that era told nigger jokes, in which the theme of inferiority played out in many ways, generally involving the dumbness of Negroes, who often mistook one word for another, or one process for another. I would hear my father tell these jokes to my uncles when they were out of hearing of their wives, or else I might hear them at a country store or a service station, places where men talked to other men. The jokes usually involved the nigger getting instructed to do something simple and making such an obvious mistake that the result was hilarious and embarrassing, and the joke served as proof that niggers were never very smart and got even the simplest facts mixed up. When we laughed at the joke, we accepted the premise.

Learning about blacks shaped my expectations. What I observed about black people was meant to fit the frame this word created inside me, so that I would see what I was supposed to see. The space of *nigger,* once prepared in my head, would resemble that same space in the heads of all the other children who played with me, and the other children with whom they played. It was a word that organized the world, and we began to learn it at the same time that we learned to speak and walk.

The word was used in many ways, always for the same purpose, to reinforce the association between *nigger* and anything bad. When my father was angry at my mother, he would accuse her of being part nigger. People who danced with too much hip movement were doing nigger dances. Something that smelled bad smelled like a nigger. Clothing that was too loud or colorful was like something a nigger would wear. Putting on deodorant rather than bathing was a nigger bath. A house where a black family lived was a nigger shack. A white person with thick lips had nigger lips, and a person with kinky hair had nigger hair. An unruly child might be called wild as a nigger, while a slothful adult was as common as a nigger, or as sorry as one. Certain kinds of flamboyance, like a penchant for lawn ornaments or a taste for bright colors, were described as niggerish. If a house fell into bad repair it was a place not even fit for a nigger to live in, a truly terrible abode. If food was particularly poor in quality, it was something even a nigger wouldn't eat. A stopgap or sloppy solution to a repair problem was a nigger rigging. In all its uses the word had a nasty, bitter edge, and, as a child, I heard the scorn and placed these feelings alongside the word, till in its final form it embodied a little of everything bad. Information and nothing more, as far as I knew. A child of three or four is not apt to question what is observed. The warp and woof of the adult world must be understood before it can be examined.

How would I have seen black people without these voices speaking in my ear? Is there were a way to know?

In the same way, by the same methods, I was taught about the weakness of girls, their place in the home, all that embodied what I was supposed to think about the opposite sex. But in the case of girls, I had access to real ones, and the evidence of what I saw and learned directly, to counterbalance what I was told. Even then, with the contradiction of real examples, some of the false information would win out over observation, and I would grow up with ideas about the weakness and inferiority of women that would later prove to be false. In the case of black people, I had only the whisperings and no direct experience, until years after my first ideas were formed.

The Fight in the Yard

——————————

I climbed down from the school bus to see my younger brother fighting a black boy in the driveway that led through a field to our house. We lived in a plain frame structure set up on cinderblocks, one grade better than a shack. It had a kitchen sink only after my father put one in. We were living in a part of the county where lower-class white people had settled, Riggstown Road, inhabited by a goodly number of Riggses and a smattering of people with other surnames.

My mother was ashamed of our house because no one had ever bothered to paint it, and because there was no bathroom, only an outhouse. We had come down in the world since my father lost his arm. But this place was better than the place we lived before, an old country store, one big open room with a counter running down the middle, that would later become Willa Romley's Fish Market. Our new house had four rooms, a back porch, and had never been used as a store. It had an electric water pump instead of a hand pump, and soon my father planned to install a sink.

September was the season for the grading and sale of cured tobacco, and my mother, to make money, had taken a truckload of dried tobacco into our house. My mother and father did this, I should say, since he was as glad to have my mother earning money as she was. The tobacco belonged to a farmer named Riggs, a drinking buddy of Daddy's. To grade tobacco, a person broke the twine that held the fistfuls of leaves to the pole on which they had hung to dry, piling the leaves on the ground, a process that released all the dried dirt and mud from the leaves into the air. Then one sorted dried tobacco, separating the golden, unblemished leaves from the brown or mottled, gathering the stems of leaves together and tying them in bundles shaped a bit like broom ends, one leaf wrapped around the top of the bunch to hold the stems fast. The front two rooms of our house were filled with dried tobacco, the smell unmistakable, pungent and dusty.

The children on the school bus saw that there was a black boy in our driveway, fighting with my little brother. No one on the bus said anything, as I recall. My sister and I clambered onto the dry grass beside the mailbox and the bus pulled away.

I stood at the end of the driveway, not certain of what I should think or do. There was a nigger boy in our yard and an old nigger woman in our house, along with pallets of dried tobacco and dust. The facts collided as if the one caused the other. I cannot remember whether this thought was explicit in my head. But it is certain that I used the word *nigger* in my thinking about the little boy and the old woman.

My brother and the black boy were fighting each other as if by instinct, without any words or any cause. I walked past them to put away my schoolbooks, then came back to see what was going on. Mother and the black woman were sitting near the open front door to catch the breeze and to keep an eye on the front yard. Mother introduced me to the black woman, but I cannot remember her name. She was there to help meet a deadline for preparing the tobacco for market. Between them was the pile of mottled leaves and, behind that, a high rectangular stack of cured tobacco tied to what we called tobacco sticks—long, thin poles of rough wood. The leaves when green and sticky with tar were tied to these sticks for hanging inside heated curing barns. When dried, the leaves ranged in color from bright yellow to rich gold to burnt black. My mother and this stranger woman made a set wage for taking the tobacco off the sticks and grading its quality so the best golden leaves could be sold for the highest price.

So many layers of this moment can be seen only now, when I look backward: that my mother and the black woman were engaged in the toxic business of making cigarettes, that they were breathing tobacco dust as they sorted the leaves, that my mother had worked in fields and on farms with black people for many years. But she was uncomfortable now. I saw this in her face and in the way she sat in the chair.

I had no experience of black people, and now here was this woman with her grandson. Maybe she called him her grandboy. She might have nodded and said, "That's my grandboy out yonder," nodding toward the young 'un. In the dialect of Jones County this last part might have sounded like "ow chonder," as in, "Thass my granbo-ey ow chonder." Vowels were stretched so that a long vowel sound might make up two spoken syllables. A black speaker would have curled the vowels one way and a white speaker would have curled them another.

I was six years old. The memory is dim, and I cannot remember whether I called the boy a nigger to his face while he and my brother circled each other, or whether my brother did, or whether anyone did. Maybe this was why they were fighting. The best memory I have is that nothing was said, and the fight simply started, the two boys being of a similar age, circling each other like two kittens with their backs raised, then colliding.

It is doubtful that the word was said aloud, in fact, since my mother would not have allowed us to say it, especially in front of a black woman with whom she was working. That woman, old and hard-skinned, clear of eye, had no reason to accept such language from us in the first place. She knew that we were as low on the social scale as she and her grandson, and even if we were white and thus enjoyed a certain kind of status denied to her, she could have still objected. Perhaps she would not have articulated such a thought, but it was surely there. She sat in the open front door with my mother, but a wall of difference separated them.

I could only see the color of her skin, the way she sat in the chair with her legs spread, skirt draped over them, a pile of dried leaves in her lap. The idea of a difference between her skin and mine was already planted in me, and in looking backward at this memory I am tempted to read the moment only for its racial content, the fact that this was my earliest moment of close contact with a black person, even though black people lived all around me. For this woman as much as for my mother, this moment was more about survival than anything else. They could earn money of their own if they would tolerate each other and work together. So they did.

I had learned already to see the world in terms of many types of difference, but particularly between rich and poor, black and white, decent and not. Country people made a life's work of deciding who was better than whom and what was better than what. Judged were individuals, families, members of families, churches, members of churches, denominations, villages, towns, makes of automobile, ways of canning, recipes for slaw, and on and on. The world was a grand hierarchy of such rankings. When necessary, the process of judgment could be bloody and mean. I would never entirely force that process—that need to decide who was above and who was below—out of my thinking, and it would be a long time before I even tried.

White Nigger

———————————

I was not to use the word *nigger,* my mother told me, because it was an ugly word and its use would mark me as common.

I must have said the word to earn this scolding, but I have no recollection of the context. The lesson was not an attempt to teach me tolerance but rather to shift my language to a path that would help me and our family to raise ourselves from the level of the poorest whites to something better.

Most white Southerners in the present will make a similar kind of statement, of course, as proof that they were raised to practice a certain level of tolerance. Nearly every white person I have spoken to about this time has uttered some variation of the statement, "We were not allowed to use the word *nigger* in my family." One should remember that most Southern mothers also proscribed such words as *shit, fuck,* and *cunt,* often to no effect whatsoever. A mother's admonition that certain language was bad only made that language appear more attractive and more useful. The prohibition against the word *nigger* had little to do with ideas of equality, and everything to do with standards of politeness.

Nigger was not a polite word but a coarse one. Good white people used other names for black people in conversation, reserving *nigger* for moments of deeper contempt. In polite company one spoke of colored people, or Negroes, though this word was more used in writing than in speech. The long vowels felt uncomfortable on the white Southern tongue. There was also the feeling that colored people, in wishing to be called Negroes, might be getting above themselves.

My mother taught me that the word *niggra,* was more acceptable. It was a kind of compromise.

(Many years after I was grown, in the mid-1980s, a white Southern boss of mine noted that he failed to see why coloreds wanted to be called blacks when the word *Negro* was so much nicer. I pointed out to him that he was saying he preferred to call this group of people black in Latin rather than in plain English. This was our last discussion of race.)

Women who wished to be thought of as decent were not allowed to use bad language. They must avoid cuss words, sexual references, and name-calling. My mother, wishing to better herself and her children, behaved like the people she met when she started to go to church. Churchwomen never said cuss words, never called names, and never used the word *nigger* in polite speech.

"Is *nigger* a bad word?" Maybe I asked this question. Maybe she gave her lesson for another reason. I picture her in the kitchen of one of the many houses we lived in, the room white-walled, probably plaster, scrubbed of stains when we moved in, though not repainted. Plastic curtains of some floral pattern hung at the windows, bought in New Bern at the Montgomery Ward store. I picture this as Sunday morning, with my mother dressing me for Sunday School. She had no clothes of a kind she could wear to church herself, but she sent my sister and me to church with a neighbor who came to pick us up in his truck.

"It's not a nice word," my mother answered. "Nice people don't say it."

"Why not?"

"Because it's not polite."

There was a further part of the explanation. I cannot remember whether my mother said this herself, but I heard it more than once from other people. "Colored people are not all the same," a white person would say. "There are white niggers, too, and they're just as trashy and low as the black ones."

Spoken of in this fashion, *nigger* was supposed to describe a way of life and not a skin color, someone trashy and common, someone whose children ran naked in the yard, who didn't bathe or keep the house clean, someone with no sense of decency. Someone who was just barely human. There were white people like this, too, or so the story went.

"White people who are like that are even worse than niggras." Perhaps my mother said this. If so, she did not need to explain further. By then I understood. Since white people were naturally superior, to lose one's decency as a white person was like jumping off a much higher cliff.

The cognitive trick involved was simple but powerful. The bad qualities that were attributed to the lowest class of white people were considered to be the normal qualities of a nigger. In general, as I had learned, white people were good and decent, though some of them came from bad stock, or went bad for other reasons. Whereas, in general, black people were bad, though some of them might learn to be better.

A white person who lived in a dirty house, who took no pride in his own hygiene, who kept his family living at an animal level, was said to be as low as a nigger, or some other similar phrase. A black person who kept himself and his house clean, had pride in his appearance, and took care of his family was trying to be like a white person. This was reasoning that a child could easily compass. Once grasped, it reordered the world. A good Negro was the exception to the rule, and the same was true of a bad white person. This neat construction explained the outliers in both races, the ones who did not fit the pattern. All evidence obtained thereafter supported the idea of white superiority almost without effort. Once the trick was taught, perceived exceptions to the racial stereotypes could be dealt with in real time.

I never heard any white person actually referred to as a nigger, not in any context, though I would hear the "white nigger" explanation over and over again. I can recall hearing a white person explain this concept very patiently to a black person, in a friendly tone, as if it made the insult all right. Someone, sometime, had invented this tale of the white nigger as a justification for the word, and I expect it is still a commonplace of the white South.

Whether or not my mother repeated this tale to me, I accepted her explanation in general and understood that she was trying to tell me something about the world. At least, I was seeing something beyond the simple lesson. She preferred that I speak politely and nicely and use words that were well approved. She wanted me to understand that reality was more complicated than I knew. To the degree that either of us understood the world, we both meant well. But in offering this explanation she underscored a layer of discomfort in herself. Whether she intended it or not, she left me with the message that there was something wrong with the way the world talked about colored people.

Divinely White

In church I learned that black was the color of sin, and white the color of purity.

Church was important to my mother, for whom it had provided a support throughout her childhood, and by associating herself with church people, she found a means of escaping the poverty in which she spent her early life. She was the only churchgoer in her immediate family, drawn to the clean interior of the sanctuary and the well-kept members of the congregation, who dressed for Sunday with care and who took pride in themselves in a way that enabled my mother to do the same. She became a member of the denomination called Church of God, attended Sunday services whenever her parents allowed, and grew up as a devout Christian.

In Jones County, she sent my sister and me to Sunday School as soon as we were old enough to ride with a neighbor, who stopped at our house on Riggstown Road and picked us up on Sunday mornings. At the time, my mother lacked Sunday clothes for herself and our family had no car in which she might have driven us. We attended Lee's Chapel United Methodist church, a very old congregation and a very small one. We rode in the pickup truck of a farmer who traveled to services by himself. At Sunday School we studied Bible stories and memorized verses, and afterward in the official church service, we listened to a preacher who talked more about the Bible from the pulpit, a height that seemed impossibly high and far away to me at that age. He appeared to stand between heaven and me.

In church, I learned that I could be washed as white as snow by giving myself to Christ, but that if I failed to take him into my heart I would be consumed by the blackness of sin. I had the choice between falling into darkness or turning to the light. The reward for embracing the brightness of heaven was eternal life, streets of gold, many mansions, choirs of angels. Along with darkness would come a lake of fire, eternal torment, the gnashing of teeth.

The lessons of church applied to the world at large, and the church reflected the world in many ways. Like all else in my early world, churches were segregated by skin color, but the stratification they provided went beyond this. The protestant denominations themselves were arranged in a kind of hierarchy, with the best people belonging to the Presbyterian church, the second best being Methodist, the Southern Baptist church being of less prestige, the Free Will Baptist churches a further step down, and the Holiness Church, or Church of God, serving the least of the white people, the ones who brought electric guitars into church, who found and cast out demons from one another on a regular basis, and who appealed to those who lived in the poorest parts of the county.

My friend Marianne was an Episcopalian, a denomination so refined there was only one small church dedicated to its worship services in the whole of Jones County.

The lessons about the purity guaranteed by whiteness, the pollution caused by any taint of blackness, crossed these denominations. The Christian Bible depicted God's son as a white-wooled lamb, God's adversary as a prince of air and darkness, salvation as a cleansing that leads to shining whiteness. God, Christ, and all the angels wore white. Death and sin were robed in black. God lived in a heaven that was always shining. The devil dwelt in the dark.

So I understood that white and black were polar opposites in many senses, not simply in terms of appearance but also of meaning and quality.

At six years old, I was hardly equipped to question the words I heard spilled into the air high above my head in the Lee's Chapel sanctuary. Church was like nothing else in my life. People sat attentively in pews, stood up at intervals with hymn books in hand and sang, closed their eyes in prayer, and deferred to the thundering lessons about the Bible that the minister broadcast from the pulpit. The subjects dealt with the largest of lessons—that the world had been created by God some time ago, that Eve brought sin into the world by conversing with a snake, that God once destroyed all earthly creatures by means of a flood, that there were certain acts and gestures that brought me into closer touch with the purpose of the world. That God so loved me that he gave his only begotten son. That everything would come to an end in a great cataclysm of beasts, earthquakes, apocalyptic horsemen, and stars falling from the sky.

Lee's Chapel sat among pines and sycamores about halfway between Pollocksville and Maysville, along Highway 17. The church was older than the highway though not older than the road the highway had replaced; the building included a tiny sanctuary to which an equally tiny Sunday School building had been added in recent times. My sister and I attended both Sunday School and church, the two hours of Sunday service stretching into an eternity. The congregation shared its preacher with the Methodist church in Pollocksville, so that he preached one sermon in the village and another at Lee's Chapel. I doubt that there were more than thirty or forty congregants in attendance on Sundays, even in those days, but to me the crowd seemed enormous. As I walked through the gathered adults, bearing a child's invisibility, I could hear them discussing the preacher, who was held to be a good speaker, with the fire of God in his words. The adults spoke of many subjects quite out of my reach, but I took something comforting from their presence, from their acceptance of my quiet listening.

One Sunday, so intent was I on wandering the churchyard during the interval between Sunday School and the main service, I forgot to go inside the church when the others did, and played outside for the whole of the hour, missing the sermon altogether. After that, I learned to pay better attention to the cues.

A few years later at another church, while waiting for service to begin, I heard the owner of the Pollocksville restaurant say, "If God had meant black people and white people to mix he would have made them one color." By then I understood better than to believe such an assertion, since blacks and whites were mixing at school with no ill effect that I could see. But if a man could say those words at such a time, and use the churchyard as his vehicle for a conversation on the subject, then the same might have happened in the Lee's Chapel congregation, before I was old enough to know what he meant.

God himself ordained that black and white people were unequal and were never to mix in any way. He had made this stipulation in order to preserve the unique purity of whiteness. Like the Israelites of old, we were his chosen people, and the world he had created belonged to us above any claim that others might have on it. I understood all this from such an early age that I cannot recall when the lesson began. But I can be relatively certain where the lesson began: during church, listening to what was said by adults, either from the pulpit or in the yard. Mixed in with lessons of obvious virtue. While I learned that I should do unto others as I would have them do unto me, while I learned that I should turn the other cheek when harmed or insulted, I absorbed the teaching that black people were a race unto themselves. I came to see black as the opposite of white in terms of the inner quality of people as well as the hue of their skin. I would only change this view years later, when in sixth grade I came face-to-face with Rhonda, Ursula, and Violet.

My lessons in racism, therefore, came to me as part of my training in goodness. So tangled was this message that I would be years in making sense of it.

The process of teaching that defined black as the opposite of white continued far beyond the walls of the church. That opposition became one of the patterns that enabled me to sort through the world. From television I understood that good cowboys wear white hats while bad guys wear black ones. From fantasy I learned that white magic is positive, black magic is evil. Loving the light, I learned that I should fear the dark.

From every side, during every movie, every television show, in the pages of every book, came images that reinforced the code. A bride married in a white dress, and the whiteness stood for purity, for virginity, for innocence, for newness. A widow draped herself in black from head to toe. Black as death, we say, black as night, black as coal, which burns red and orange. Black as sin. Black is an abyss into which we fear to fall.

To follow a dark path. To walk in the shadows. When we

were with God we were in green pastures, beside still waters. Our peril was the valley of the shadow of death. God was a light we carried with us. God repelled the dark. The light was supreme because God was supreme. White was supreme because the light was white. Blackness could never be bright.

Lucifer fell from the light into a pit of darkness. Satan fell from white to black.

Savagery was darkness, and darkness was savagery, in which people and nations could become lost. Dark ages were times of chaos and ignorance. To emerge from such a period required rebirth and enlightenment. Blackness consumed, whiteness illuminated.

A room painted in total blackness was a cave, a grave, a pit, a dungeon, forbidding, gloomy, gothic, wrong. A room painted all in white passed without notice.

Cleanliness was whiteness. Dirt was dark. Good triumphed over evil. White won out over black.

These symmetries were built into the images, in the language, in the background of consciousness, foretold everywhere. Simply reversing the color scheme produced nonsense. One could not speak of ignorance sweeping over a people like a tide of brightness. The phrase merely puzzled. The antagonism of black and white shaped the world of meaning inside my head, and black bore the negative value in all cases.

To view a situation as black and white produced an expedient clarity; all other views resulted in the confusion of gray, the realism of the murk.

Even when I understood that I had made certain assumptions about whiteness and blackness, I continued to employ the metaphors because the language insisted that I do. The pairing of whiteness with virtue and blackness with negatives was too useful in the making of metaphor to abandon. Dark comedy, blackguards, the dark arts, realms of shadow, a cloud crossing the sun, a shadow falling over a face in a film. Darkness was menace, fear, uncertainty, chaos, a harbinger of endings. Blackness was blindness, the loss of movement, the space of nightmare. I would turn to the light for hope. I would confront the dark to face my fears.

All this had begun in the simple notion that white was good, and black was not. Evidence accumulated, white as snow, dark as soot. I saw what I was meant to see.

Good Old Boy

One morning, not long after we moved from Riggstown Road to a house on Island Creek Road, I found my father in the kitchen with my mother as she tended to cuts on his face. I could smell the sharp scent of the open bottle of merthiolate on the kitchen table, sitting next to a tin pan full of water and some cloths colored with pink and red. My father's eye was swollen and a small gash, diagonal to his eyebrow, oozed dark blood. They were speaking quietly, in short sentences. Their words were something like this:

"Is it still bleeding?" my father asked.

"Little bit," Mama said. "You might need stitches."

"I ain't going to any damn doctor." Daddy set his jaw and knotted his brows. "Just put the merthiolate on it like I told you."

"Hold pressure to it," Mama said. "Get the bleeding to slow."

He grunted and took one of the cloths, pressing it to the wound. The kitchen was quiet a while. Mama stirred to make coffee, bringing him a cup from the percolator pot. When he took it to drink, she held the cloth to his eye. By then the oozing had slowed to thick drops.

She lifted the bottle of merthiolate. "You ready?"

"Yeah. Go ahead."

She looked at him carefully. If she hurt him with the merthiolate he might slap her just because she was the one who put it on the cut. He was like that, my father. "You want me to fan it? It's going to sting."

"Shit, no," he said, and she painted the cut while he sat there, stoic. He was a man, the pain was nothing to him. That would be his reaction this time. His posture told me this.

No one had lived in this house for a long time, nor can I remember anyone living there after we moved out. The place had been abandoned by its owner and looked to be falling down, set in an empty field near the edge of the wide, dark Croatan National Forest; the top story was boarded up, unlivable. We lived in the four downstairs rooms.

There was no heat in the house when we moved in, so Daddy installed a small space heater, open flame, purchased from the place where he worked, Jenkins Gas Company. This was a new job for him, and so there was little money in the family that winter, and we were eating potatoes, nothing but potatoes, the only food we could afford.

These details matter because the poverty and the threat of hunger made my father angry. I could see the anger in the set of his jaw, sense it in his deep, sullen quiet.

Now he sat in the kitchen with a bruised face and cuts over one eye.

He had been out all night and returned with wounds. When he lay down in his bed to sleep, I asked my mother what happened.

"He got in a fight, I guess," she said.

"Where?"

"Maybe somewhere in Richlands, he don't want to say." She was pumping water at the sink, the old hand pump rusty and creaking. There was no plumbing in this house, other than the pump and the drain. "Maybe somewhere in Hatchville. Him and his friends."

Hatchville was one of the places where black people lived, a stripe of houses on either side of Highway 58 at the crossroads with Highway 17. There were other black neighborhoods in or near Pollocksville, these being the Heights, a cluster of houses on a rise of land across from the sawmill; the Back Streets, inside the village limits of Pollocksville; and Murphytown, a stretch of brick houses along Highway 17. Black families were scattered through other parts of the county, too.

We kept quiet that day, and Daddy stayed sober when he woke up, looking more thoughtful than usual, sitting in the living room, smoking cigarettes and watching a western on the television.

White men gathered wherever they could to drink and raise a bit of hell on a Friday or Saturday night. Black men, no doubt, did the same. This was what a good old boy was expected to do. In Pollocksville, there were only a few places to have fun, and the pool hall was one of them. Since the sale of liquor by the drink was illegal in North Carolina, public drinking took on a sinful, shadowy taint, regardless of its circumstances. People here did not drink in restaurants, and even if such a practice had been legal, there was only one such eating place in Pollocksville, the Trent Restaurant, where respectable people ate chicken pastry and country-fried steak and sipped nothing stronger than sweet iced tea.

The local pool hall, called simply that, and not even distinguished by a sign as far as I can recall, took the place of a bar. For this reason it had a bad reputation. There were clubs of various kinds in the larger towns in the larger counties around ours, but in Jones County, there were few places where a man could drink in peace. Even at the pool hall, a man generally brought his own liquor and kept it in his truck or on his person, wrapped in a paper bag.

The pool hall was also the rumored central location for the local Ku Klux Klan, though it was too small for meetings, which were supposedly held on the upper floor of Mr. Paul

Armstrong's general goods store. This was, at any rate, the local gossip. The man who owned the pool hall also owned a service station next door. He was a sullen fellow with an artificial leg and a well-known hatred for black people. Exactly how he earned this reputation was a matter of mystery, though it was natural to guess that he was part of the Klan.

My father's fight would likely have had something to do with the pool hall and the good old boys who were its patrons. He was friendly with the men who hung out there, and might have begun a night of drinking thereabouts. At some point he and his friends would have decided to look for trouble, and found it. They would hardly have questioned their own motives since this kind of behavior was expected of men of their kind. The fight that night was not likely to have been anything official, or to have involved white sheets or hoods, or to have had any real purpose other than to pass the time. The fight might not have involved black people at all.

Over a few days my father's cut healed, and whatever story he might have told about the fight remained unspoken. Such was his temper that if I had asked him about it I was as likely to make him angry as to get an answer, and there was never any accounting for how angry he became.

In recalling this memory I have presumed that this moment of violence had some connection to black people. At least in part this is a fictive assumption, meaning that I am forcing the connection beyond my memory. I cannot recall the exact conversation between my parents that morning. My father was in every case a violent man, and I remember the unfamiliar sensation of his calm that morning, the fight having burned away his anger. Whether or not he had been fighting a black man or a white man on that occasion, he was part of a system from which violence could be extracted at any moment.

Black people called my father Captain Jack, though he had never served in the army or held any rank. At the time I simply thought this a polite mode of address, perhaps a mark of respect that my father had earned. As a man who delivered bottled gas to people's houses, and later as a refrigeration and air-conditioning specialist, he moved constantly among black people, hooking up big steel bottles of gas to cooking stoves in houses throughout the county, repairing refrigerators and freezers for anyone who could pay. He had little or nothing to say on most subjects, and I never heard him express an opinion about segregation, integration, politics, or even television shows, except on occasion to look at the TV screen in disgust and say, "Turn that goddamn shit off." Whatever thoughts he had, he kept to himself, almost to the point of pathology.

But he and his friends were the men who would have been called on, in earlier times and perhaps in these, to ignite together in mobs, to burn crosses or houses or both, to hang black men without benefit of trial. Perhaps he was called on to do so in his own time, and I never knew. It would not surprise me to learn that this was true. His store of anger would have been sufficient to such a task. All he would have required was a few friends to back him up and a reason to act.

I would only have known the personal edge of this at the time, the fact that my father, and the men around me, were all kings of their castles, empowered to act as they saw fit in their houses and on their land. I would only have known that living with my father was like living with a fire that could barely be controlled. But later I would learn about all the cruelties and inhumanities of slavery and Jim Crow, including lynchings, rapes, beatings, torture, forced labor, and much more; and later still I would understand these atrocities had been practiced in Jones County and in the region around me at one time or another. Practiced by people much like those I knew. By men like my father and his drinking buddies, by good folk like those with whom I went to church. By people like me.

Johnny Shiloh

O n Sunday nights I lay on the linoleum floor in front of the television and watched *The Wonderful World of Disney,* a practice so regular it took on the form of ritual. Disney could be relied on to provide the same kind of entertainment week after week, child-oriented stories full of sentiment and heart-warming treacle, often featuring a beloved horse or dog or other pet. On one such night in the early 1960s, I watched a movie called *Johnny Shiloh,* and this began my education in the Civil War.

Johnny Shiloh offered up the story of a boy from Ohio who ran away from home to join the Union army, a retelling of the life of John Joseph Klem, who left home at age eleven to serve in Mr. Lincoln's army. In the movie, Johnny pestered the adult soldiers into accepting him, demonstrated his pluck by undergoing the same training in arms as any soldier in his unit, and served with bravery at the Battle of Shiloh. He was later captured by Confederate soldiers and befriended by a boy his own age; and he escaped in time to warn his superior officers of Southern troop movements. He was a child who saved the day, a theme repeated over and over in the lore of Disney.

I fell into the story for ninety minutes, enthralled at the notion that a boy my own age could earn the respect of manly men like Brian Keith, one of the male leads. Johnny's capture by the Confederate army would have had me on the edge of my seat had I not been lying on the floor at the time. His friendship with the red-haired Southern boy overwhelmed me with a desire for a friendship of my own. At the end of the movie I wanted to be Johnny myself. "He sure wanted to help out President Lincoln," I said.

"He did," my mother agreed.

"I think those Rebs didn't have any business fighting against the president like that. They couldn't win anyway."

My mother gave me one of her disdainful looks. "Well, you wouldn't have thought so at the time."

"Why not?"

She pursed her lips. "Because back then we would have been on the other side."

The mild rebuke gave me pause, since my mother rarely made assertions of that kind. She was hinting at a knowledge of the past that she declined to share. But her words did nothing to dint the romantic connection I felt to the story of Johnny Shiloh, including his loyalty to Abraham Lincoln, his passion for preserving the Union, and his contempt for the Rebs. The Rebs were the Confederates, I supposed. As for the notion that the Rebs were my people, I had no real understanding of what she meant. In the movie, the Confederates were the bad guys. Why would I be on the side of the bad guys?

Still, she left me with the impression that I had failed in my understanding in some way. She herself merely found it amusing to a degree.

My response amounted to nothing more than my romance with the notion of being Johnny Shiloh, standing at the center of adult attention, the boy about whom everyone around him cared. The movie scarcely dealt with the real themes of the Civil War, its terms reduced to support for or antipathy toward Mr. Lincoln, whom Johnny so revered. The issue of slavery hardly came up.

But I had only weakly identified with a profound story, the idea of the fallen South and the glory of yesterday, that should have enthralled me. The past had failed to make some essential connection with me. I had no sympathy with the idea of plantations, or rich people owning slaves, or Southern belles, or patrician gentlemen, or any of the trappings of that older time. In fact, I had scarcely any knowledge of that past. What little I had learned made me skeptical of the things I was supposed to think. What history textbooks had taught me about slavery, cursory as it was, made me think it was a bad thing. What I understood about the Civil War made me certain that the good guys had won.

The Shoe Man

Commerce in Pollocksville had been dying slowly since the advent of the automobile, which gave people the ability to shop in New Bern or Kinston, where the stores were bigger and the discounts more frequent. I have mentioned most of the businesses in town, the largest being the gas company, the oil company, the school supply warehouse, and what was called a candy company, though it served more as a distributor of various kinds of dry goods. From this business, each summer, I bought a new pair of tennis shoes.

Along the highways, at various intersections, were family-run grocery stores, some with a gas pump, most of them slowly going broke. My mother ran one of those stores along Highway 17, eking out a bit of extra money selling pop and candy and some food items, around the time my brother was born. We lived in the house behind the storefront. My father was jealous of my mother and accused her of cheating on him with various men who came to the store, including some of the salesmen, and the store wasn't making much money anyway. So Mama closed it and we moved again.

Some businesses were segregated and some were not, prior to 1964. The motel was for white people only, as was the restaurant. Black hair and white hair being different, there were barbershops and beauty parlors for each. General stores and country stores were sometimes segregated and sometimes not, depending on the attitude and reputation of the store's owner. White people rarely patronized businesses owned by black people, especially when there was a white alternative at hand.

One exception in our village was the shoe-repair shop in Hatchville.

The first time I went there, in the company of my mother, I would have been in school, no earlier than fourth grade, as far as I recall. Now that I was growing more slowly, I wore my one pair of good shoes longer, and often wore out the soles. My father's Sunday shoes occasionally needed a new heel, and perhaps he wore out a sole or two, though he spent most of his time in work boots that simply had to be replaced from time to time. My sister had penny loafers that required stitching at the back and new soles. Being frugal, Mother often took new shoes to the shoe man for taps to be put on the heels, not to provoke us to dance but rather to give the heel and tip of the shoe a longer wear.

Hatchville was a small, unincorporated village of black people at the junction of two main roads. The houses in Hatchville sat close to the road on both sides, some in good repair and well kept, some unpainted or falling down, a mix of the old style of swept-dirt yard with the new style of grassy carpet. Some small streets ran through the settlement, though I do not remember these with any clarity. In some places there were two or more rows of houses, the interior street almost hidden.

The shoe shop appeared much like a house on the outside, weathered clapboard or brown shingle, something like that, raised on pillars of cinderblocks a couple of feet above the ground. I expect there was a sign outside, but I can't remember it. Inside, the building had an unfinished feeling, walls of unpainted board, signs hand-lettered, neat but homemade. Shelves on the walls held rows of shoes, either used and for sale or repaired and awaiting pickup by their owners, all shining brightly, renewed and hopeful. The room smelled of shoe polish, sharp and musky.

In one part of the store the shoe man had built a long counter to house his iron shoe forms, heavy scissors, the machine for leather stitching, shoe brushes, electric polisher, and cloths to polish and shine. He could remake a battered old shoe to a state that was almost new, excepting the creases in the leather. A comfortable shoe, life extended, pleasing to both thrift and pride. A man could get by owning only one pair of good shoes with a good cobbler like the shoe man at hand.

I cannot remember his name, nor whether my mother called

him by name when she brought him shoes to be mended. I remember some outline of their talk, simple and polite. "How do, ma'am?" he'd ask.

"I'm just fine, just fine," she'd reply.

"So you brought me some work?"

"That's right." She opened the shopping bag she carried and told him what kind of work she wanted done on each shoe, laying them on the counter. He picked them up from there, examined them, put them back.

He was a short, stocky man with a serious air, direct and plain. He and my mother spoke to each other politely, and I recall no subservience in his behavior, only a bit of distance. He was brisk and precise. I suspect he was reserved with all his customers, and since he was in his own shop and had a monopoly on the shoe-repair trade in our part of the county, he commanded respect. He was a craftsman and a business-man whose store was one of the places where black and white people crossed paths. When my mother spoke of him, she said something like, "That man can make a shoe look like you just bought it at a store."

She might have said those words outside the shop, or per-haps in the car as we were preparing to turn around in the dirt parking lot beside the building.

For some reason, I can remember that moment most vividly, the glimpse of Hatchville as my mother backed the car out of its parking space and turned onto the highway.

Had we been on Main Street of Pollocksville, even the

quickest glimpse of the street on such a day would bring a face, a person I recognized, perhaps even knew by name, or else some idle recognition of this building or that one. By those years my family had moved from one house to another maybe a half dozen times, and we had known neighbors in several neighborhoods, moving from Riggstown to another former tobacco grading house, then to another house on Highway 17. We had seen by face a fair portion of the county. On Main Street in my village, only a half mile or so from where I was, I would have recognized someone.

But that day on the main street of Hatchville, I recognized no one at all, and knew nothing of the buildings that I saw. Several black people stood near doorways, worked in yards behind picket fences, fed chickens at the back of their houses, as my mother turned our car onto the road and drove back to the intersection. I knew not one face, though I had driven along that part of the highway dozens of times. In essence , the people of Hatchville were invisible to me.

Invisible describes that feeling only partly, in fact. In my world black people were hardly present at all, even on that day, even after a visit to the shoe man in the shoe shop. No part of my brain had been trained to see black faces or to try to know them. No mechanism of recognition or interest was present. I see this only in retrospect, when I reach for a memory and find a blank instead. At the time, I saw only shapes that I remember as people, but I had no need to know who they were, felt no curiosity, and was, in fact, more interested in the repairs to my shoes. I did not, after all, bother to know the shoe man's name.

I had accepted that black people were different from me and entirely separate from me. This idea of separation had become so complete that in later years I might live in a house in sight of black people who were neighbors and never see them at all. Yet at any time, riding down any road in the county, I knew the places where the white people lived and could have named the families in many of the houses, at least those in the part of Jones County nearest Pollocksville.

The year was 1964, or maybe a year later. The world was soon to change.

The Uncomfortable Dark

Some of the children at our white elementary school in Pollocksville were brown-skinned all along. Manny Potter was the child I remember best. His skin was olive, his hair shiny and thick, silky and straight, his eyes black as coals. He was handsome, the darling of the pale-skinned boys partly because he had failed second grade and was older than the rest of us, and partly because he sat loosely in his chair, offered little respect or deference to the teachers, and drew excellent pictures of naked women in his notebook during class. In his art he displayed a sophisticated sense of perspective, mass, and proportion.

His family was as brown as he. I remember that he had a number of sisters, maybe a younger brother. My mother early on, in second grade, warned me to have nothing to do with him. When I asked why, she said without hesitation that he was too brown. I asked whether he was a nigger and she said no. I asked what was he, and she said maybe he was a Mexican or maybe he was Indian or maybe some of both. But whatever he was, I should keep my distance from him.

He made a strong impression on me when he was in the room with the rest of us, but that might be true because he was handsome and I liked to look at him. There was nothing disruptive about his behavior except that he was essentially indifferent to what the teachers had to say, as if he knew all along that school was not for him. He preferred to draw his pencil sketches, or to snicker with the other boys about the girls or the teacher or the fart he had just released. He impressed them by his skill at farting silently, signaling that he was doing so by lifting one buttock from the chair. The others would pucker their noses as if smelling something foul, and some would giggle, and the teacher would call them down, with Manny all the while sitting there deadpan.

What I knew of him came from glimpses, seeing his siblings playing in the yard when they lived on Highway 58 near Piney Grove Road, or glimpsing what he drew in his notebooks as I walked to the pencil sharpener. I recall that his clothes were different from those of the other boys, that he wore jeans less, and what we would have called trousers more, the clothes and shirts sometimes tight, as if they were hand-me-downs.

Like my family, his lived in various houses around Pollocksville, and when I was in sixth grade or thereabout his family moved into a house where my family had once lived, a place with the old detached kitchen still standing, separated from the main house by a porch, though no longer used as a kitchen.

My father had a business next door to that house, a brick building in which he repaired refrigerators and freezers and sometimes sold new ones. I was aware of Manny and his siblings since I sat in my father's shop to answer the phones, coming there after school and on Saturdays during the school year, and all day in the summer time, giving my mother relief from the job.

Manny mowed the lawn in tight trousers, no shirt, wearing no underwear, a clear sign that he was dangerous.

Manny's sister was thin, pretty in her way, dark-haired, wearing loose cotton dresses, tentative in her approach. I met her one day when I came out of my father's shop to escape the tedium, to rest my eyes from whatever science-fiction novel I was reading at the time. I made friends with girls much more easily than with boys, so I said hello and we talked a while, a conversation that started in a halting way, something like this:

"You know my brother?"

"Manny used to be in my class at school."

"He doesn't go to school no more."

"I know. Do you?"

"I used to but I quit. I got too tired of it. We move around a lot."

"So do we," I said.

"You have to sit in that place all day?" She indicated the building, Jack's Refrigeration Service, my father's business.

"I have to answer the phone," I said. "People call my daddy to fix their air conditioners."

"I wish we had an air conditioner."

I'm sure she told me her name and I told her mine. We talked for a while, about the weather, the heat, our favorite shows on television. The conversation moved from hesitancy to comfort. She wanted some company, she enjoyed the chatter. So did I.

Across the street from us, out of the Jenkins Gas Company building, came one of the women who worked in the office there, and she began to holler at me from across the road. "Jimmy," she called, "leave that girl alone and go back inside."

Manny's sister flushed red and said nothing.

"I'm fine," I told the woman, whose name I can't recall any more than I can remember Manny's sister's name. "We're just talking."

She stood there for a moment. Perhaps she repeated her warning and I repeated my refusal. She grew angry at me for not listening and soon went back into the air-conditioned building. Manny's sister and I talked for a bit longer, mostly about our outrage at the interference from the woman across the street. Manny's sister was clearly embarrassed, and we shortly separated. Maybe we thought we had won that moment. But we never spoke again.

The white woman from across the street had no hesitation

in asserting herself as my protector, telling me to go back into the shop, even in front of Manny's sister. She felt responsible for me perhaps because I occasionally walked over to the gas-company office to buy a soft drink from the vending machine, or because my father had once worked for the company, or perhaps simply because we were both white. She meant to save me from something.

For Manny's sister, the moment was brutal and direct. She was dismissed as a subhuman, a creature to be avoided. No doubt she had suffered this kind of outrage before. She said nothing in particular after the moment passed, and we talked for a while longer, to show that we could defy this adult and do as we pleased. But very shortly she went back into her house, and I went back into the shop.

I thought about that moment for a long time afterward, angry at the woman across the street. Inside me was the feeling that I had done something wrong, but as it swelled I countered it with this anger, with the certainty that I had done nothing at all, that I had simply been friendly to a person who was friendly to me. The embarrassment roiled in me and I stoked it.

But I never told my mother about this moment, since I knew that she would have sided with the good white woman who worked at the gas company. She would have agreed that I should have nothing to do with the Potter family; she had already told me that years before. She would have told me not to talk to Manny's sister again.

The Maid in the Weeds

I knew of only a few people in our town who had black servants, though there were probably others. People who had maids or cooks never liked to talk about it. Even the richest people in the county pretended to be poor when speaking of money matters. None of my friends would claim to have been raised by the infamous Southern mammy who, in gothic mythology, was supposed to have loved her white family as much as her colored one.

One black person I knew who was identified as a servant to a white family was Miss Ruthie, who was my family's neighbor for a time. My mother said that Miss Ruthie had worked for the Truman family and they took care of her now. This likely meant that they helped her to go to doctor appointments or to do grocery shopping, and perhaps gave her money from time to time. She was too old to have been a servant for the Trumans when I knew her; the relationship must have been an old one.

My parents had bought a house on Barrus Street in Pollocksville next to the railroad tracks, a Jim Walker prefabricated home painted mustard yellow by the old tenants, and overpainted green when my parents bought it. We had been residents of the village rather than the surrounding countryside since a few years before, my parents marriage having settled into alternating periods of turbulence and normalcy that would mark it for a few more years, until it finally dissolved. As a family we had begun to attend the Pollocksville Baptist Church and gradually became counted among the decent white people of Jones County, our status elevated by our house-owning and churchgoing. In that tiny house we anchored ourselves and made a respectable business of our intersection, where before there had been a questionably fertile family who nearly burst the walls out.

Miss Ruthie's small, unpainted shack sat in a patch of woods behind our house, between us and the river, close enough that we could sometimes see smoke from her chimney, though the trees and undergrowth in summer were so thick that the structure was almost completely hidden. Not more than a patch of the roof could be seen. At night there was no sign of light peeping through a window, only dark leaves and shadows. In winter one might glimpse the shape of the building, given a narrow appearance by the pitch of the roof. Miss Ruthie kept to herself, my mother told me, and that was surely true.

There was a rumor she had a husband back there, but I never glimpsed him.

We only saw Miss Ruthie when she walked down her path along our yard and disappeared into her house, or sometimes when she walked along the highway. She kept her face down and her gaze focused on the ground, her expression bleak and detached, as if she had long ago seen more than she could bear. She sometimes carried a burlap sack with her, to pick up discarded soda bottles that she could return to any of the local stores for a few cents of bottle deposit money. She moved slowly, with some effort, the clearest sign of her age.

One day, as my sister and I watched through the kitchen window, Miss Ruthie appeared on the path to her house, wearing a loose house dress, her head covered, maybe in a dark straw hat. Her walk was squat and tired. She was chewing something, jaw moving, as she stepped into the knee-high weeds and broom straw. In a bar of sunlight she halted, bent her knees, and hiked up her skirt. Her rump gleamed, she squatted, and started to pee. She took her ease in the weeds, unaware that we watched until my little brother opened a window and hollered at her to stop. Startled, she straightened, took a step, let down her skirt and walked into some gap in the undergrowth that led to her house. She glanced back at our house once, I remember. I could not read her expression.

The sight of Miss Ruthie bending her knees to pee in the grass made my sister laugh, and still does when we remember it, though in fact it was not all that unusual for people to use the outdoors instead of the toilet. Our new house had an indoor toilet but this had not always been the case. Most of our early houses had an outhouse, also called a johnny house, though in fact we did not often visit the outhouse itself except to empty the slop pot that we all used. The pot was usually kept in the back room of whatever place we inhabited. A slop pot was simply a poor man's chamber pot, ours made of metal enameled with white paint, fixed with a good tight lid to control the smell. A roll of toilet paper sat beside it, the most modern concession to our hygiene.

My father was prone to pee outdoors more often than in the house, and he did so without a trace of embarrassment when working on his job. During the summers when my mother worked in tobacco crews, she did the same, and so did my siblings and I.

So the idea of peeing outdoors was not what made us laugh at Miss Ruthie.

My brother opened a window and hollered, "You better quit that!" He was gleeful at his own audacity. We were safely inside the house, at the windows. She had thought the place empty and, perhaps, learned only then that she had a new neighbor. My memory of her face is hazy, but I had seen her often enough to reconstruct the expression, startled, perhaps mildly irritated. The end of the moment remains the same as the other memory;

she looked at our house in some consternation, let down her skirt, and walked away from her puddle of pee.

Maybe it was her bare rump hovering over the grass that made us laugh, or maybe it was the stream of piss, or the fact that she wore no underclothes, only the dress. Our grandmother had the same habit, finding drawers too hot and too much trouble, preferring the comfort of her thin dress against her bare skin. But my mother had trained us to wear underclothing, always clean, always changed every day, since she was certain that small clothes were a part of civilization and the social ladder that she meant us all to climb.

I have called Miss Ruthie a maid in the title of this chapter. In fact I have no idea in what capacity she served or was connected to her white family, only that I heard of the connection more than once. I knew her by name, and I knew her face, because a prominent white family had a responsibility for her, in some fashion. Like the shoe repair man, Miss Ruthie's narrative had lifted her out of invisibility in my eyes. She had some connection to the white world and thus I had a reason to know her and to remember her. This was more important than the fact that she was our neighbor; we had lived near black families before and I had never learned their names. Miss Ruthie was one of the few black adults whom I would have recognized before the integration of public schools and the collision of the separate black and white worlds that came with it.

In the end it was that moment of watching her relieve herself in the grass at the edge of my family's backyard that made me remember her so vividly. I laughed at her in order to feel superior to her. I laughed to remind myself that she was less than me, and to reinforce that truth. She would live there, a hundred yards from my back door, for the rest of the years I lived in Jones County, and I would never speak a single word to her.

CHANGE

Integration

I n May 1968, the Supreme Court ruled that Freedom of
Choice plans, while not unconstitutional, were likely
insufficient to provide a remedy for the problem of school segregation. The court noted that the choice of what school to
attend must in fact be a free one, and that most such programs
failed this standard, since hostility between the races brought
pressure to bear that tended to keep black students in black
schools. The ruling stated, in effect, that black students were
not free to choose in the South, regardless of whether a free-
choice plan was in place. The court reaffirmed that all jurisdic-
tions had an obligation under law to take positive steps to end
the operation of dual school systems for blacks and whites. This
decision brought about the end of segregated public schools in
Jones County.

This rocked our little community, and the resentment of the adults around me was palpable. Jones County's school board made plans to consolidate the schools into one integrated system in the fall. Jones County's white people made plans to open private schools in order to avoid sending white children into schools with the black children of the county. In my town, the Pollocksville Academy was born.

Though I was aware of the hostility to integration, discussions of the issue at the adult level passed me by, and I had little inkling of the plans for the new public school system or for the private school until late in the summer. I doubt my parents were involved in these talks, since there was no possibility that my brothers, sister, or I would attend private school. My mother worked at the restaurant as a waitress and heard a good deal of gossip there, I expect, but she hardly ever shared any with her children. As usual, our family was focused on its own affairs. My father had been sober for some months, and we were attending church as a family.

There was never any discussion about where my brothers, sister, and I would attend school. We never considered the idea of private school for ourselves. The public schools were free; why pay for something that was free? Segregation was well and good, but it was not worth spending any money on it. Given this fact, there were no discussions about integration in our family, other than the occasional gossip about who would be attending private school and who would not.

The Russells, who owned the restaurant where my mother worked and the house we rented behind it, were smugly certain that their grandchildren would go to private school, and that this was the Christian choice.

Irene Miller, my sister's sometimes friend, would attend the private school.

So would Marianne, who had been my best friend for so many years. She told me at some point that summer, over the phone.

So when school started in the fall, my old, comfortable set of classmates from Alex H. White Elementary School would be scattered forever.

While I had grown accustomed to having Rhonda and Ursula as my friends, I had no personal desire to pursue integration any further. I would have stopped integration myself at that point, if I could, simply because I was afraid of change.

This was the summer in which my eyes began to open to many things. A presidential election campaign was taking place, with the president, Lyndon Johnson, on the sidelines. He had announced earlier in the year that he would not stand for reelection, and most people blamed this on the conduct of the war in Vietnam.

I had begun to watch the news more carefully, and occasionally sneaked a peek at the newsmagazines *Time* and *Newsweek* at the local drugstore. I began to read about the Vietnam War, the race riots in U.S. cities, and the coming presidential election.

The word *ghetto* entered my vocabulary. The Tet Offensive had torn the curtain off the Vietnam War and opened it to public discussion, and significant parts of the country began to oppose the war. Presidential campaigns by Eugene McCarthy, Robert Kennedy, and Hubert Humphrey played themselves out on television, along with the campaigns of Nelson Rockefeller, Richard Nixon, and George Wallace. I watched the Democratic National Convention nominate Hubert H. Humphrey as its candidate in the midst of savage violence on the Chicago streets. The Republican Convention caused less uproar but offered up Richard Nixon, whose nose was pointed like Pinocchio's, and who had eyes like lifeless buttons.

George Wallace, a segregationist, campaigned for president as a third-party candidate, and drew strong support from the white people in my county who wanted to return to legal segregation and to refuse any push toward equality with black people. He had attempted to halt the enrollment of black students at white schools in Alabama, and this had made him a hero to many. The anger at integration that had been suppressed during the years of Freedom of Choice found its voice in support of Wallace and his ideas, discussed haphazardly at the Baptist church I attended, between Sunday School classes and the preacher's endless sermon. Mr. Russell expressed his outrage that black people could now eat at the Trent Restaurant, and he was afraid the government would soon force us to attend church with black people, too. George Wallace offered hope that segregation might by some miracle continue, or, at least, he gave people a means to vote their anger.

Integration struck fear into white people because it meant the possibility of total dissolution of what we called our way of life. I sometimes heard that phrase, "our way of life," though no one was ever very specific about what it meant. It had something to do with keeping black people out of our toilets and restaurants in order to stave off the wrath of God. But we already had to eat in restaurants with black people. We already had to share public bathrooms with them. So the old way of life was already gone, wasn't it? Well, no, the government might do even more; it might force us to admit black people into our churches, or make us live next to them as neighbors. The government might encourage white women to marry black men and have black babies.

In fact, black people and white already lived as neighbors. They had already been copulating with one another, by choice and by coercion, for centuries. My own family lived next to Miss Ruthie, the woman who had peed in the grass in our backyard. In one direction from our house lay the houses of white people. In the other direction lay the houses of black people. Resistance to the idea of integration made us fear the idea of black neighbors as if this arrangement of our homes were new.

Integration implied a knitting together of many threads, the making of a cohesive whole out of diverse elements. An integrated circuit, for instance, was a single electrical circuit that performed the duties of what had before been multiple circuits. The notion of integration had about it an air of the ideal, a belief that our different colors of people could be blended into one harmonious whole. As a result, *integration* was a term that could not have frightened white people more if it had been designed to do so. In our eyes, integration assumed the white race was obsolete and would be superseded in the new order of things. And I knew it was true that black people were already threatening to get rid of us during the revolution; Rhonda and Ursula had told me so.

The substitution of desegregation for integration removed the idealism and restated the notion in practical terms. There was something realistic in the newer word, and also something diminished. A process of desegregation simply meant dissolving the legal barriers between white people and black people, and ending the provision of separate public accommodations and schools. This idea contained no bringing together of the peoples but simply tore down the walls between them that were publicly enforced. As time went by, desegregation appeared to be a better description of the process that was taking place. In the end, the lines of separation between blacks and whites merely shifted a bit to accommodate the fact that they had to share space from time to time. But in this I am referring to the white people who stayed in public schools. A large number of whites fled the school system during that first summer.

I had no idea that something like a school could be put

together so quickly. I began to hear about the Pollocksville Academy in August.

So eighth grade was to begin, for me, with many friendships broken. The life of our community was disrupted in many ways by the change. Schools were one of the mainstays of social activity for all of us. Both white and black communities had built up social rituals attached to support for their high schools, such as attending football and basketball games, dances and fundraisers. Now both races had to rebuild these separate patterns into something new and shared.

Further, what had appeared to be one race was now divided into two: those white people who would attend public schools, and those who refused.

Still, it was summer, and hot, and the fields were full of tobacco, corn, and soybeans. People fished in the rivers, made trips to the beach, attended Rotary Club meetings, and moved through the familiar patterns of their daily lives. The changes to the schools and the new rules of integration joined the quiet tide of life moving forward. The news of the school changes came in the midst of the whole of life, including my chronic health problems, my parents and their troubles, my first jobs as a babysitter, my life as a young Baptist, the growth of my first pubic hairs, and the changes in my body that came with my status as a soon-to-be teenager. The integration of schools was one part of this world, important but not all-encompassing.

The plan for school consolidation that emerged in the latter part of the summer specified that none of the county's schools were to be closed. For one more year the separate black and white high schools were to remain open. Grades one through eight were to be consolidated, their student populations split between the former black and white elementary schools in the four towns: Pollocksville, Trenton, Maysville, and Comfort. In the following year, the black high school would become a junior high school and the white high school would become the county's only high school. Both those schools were to be renamed. These plans, in their initial incarnation, showed a certain level of enlightenment. In other parts of eastern North Carolina, white high schools retained their names and mascots, and black schools were closed in favor of their white counterparts. Jones County chose its different course out of necessity, perhaps, since the county was desperately poor and lacked the funds for new school construction.

The eighth grade in Pollocksville was assigned to the J. W. Willie School, the former black elementary school located just outside of town, named for a member of a prominent local family. This school was markedly more modern than Alex H. White, which I had attended before then. The decision appears curious in hindsight, since it forced the younger children to deal with the older school, its rickety stairs and its poor access for the handicapped. We older students inherited the newer school. My teacher for the year would be Mrs. Ferguson again, as she moved to the Willie school with us. Other of our old teachers would do the same.

From eighth grade through my senior year, I would attend school as a member of the minority: black students outnumbered white students nearly two to one in the public schools of Jones County. Soon I would have a lesson in what it was like to be in the minority.

The J. W. Willie School / Bag Lunch

O n my first morning at J. W. Willie School I learned that change, no matter how necessary, could be deeply uncomfortable and unsettling.

What I remember is that the schoolyard lay flat as a table-top, and the school sat on a concrete slab on the ground, with rows of classes lined side by side, each opening onto a covered walkway. The wings of the building formed a cross. A bit of playground surrounded the school, with monkey bars and see-saws, maybe a swing set, all unused, since the younger grades who would have played on them were now attending my old school. The upper grades, five through eight, occupied the Willie School, and we were far too old to do anything on monkey bars except drape ourselves against them in as cool a fashion as we could manage.

The building felt alien and strange, sitting so low to the

ground, bringing the outside world so close to the classroom. At Alex H. White we had been raised up from the ground, protected by interior hallways, removed from the trees and lawn, looking down on them from what felt like a great height. That had been an older building, a different idea about the relationship between the classroom and the world, imposing, occupying a central place in the village. The Willie School was more modern, simpler in design, a different way of relating to the outdoors.

In the early heat of that first morning, students milled about the yard, in and out of the classrooms. Most of them were strangers to me. Most of them were black. I had not gone to school with strangers in years, nor I had been in a space before where black people outnumbered white people. From the first moment, standing in front of the school, I could feel the difference as a kind of fear inside me. Strangers were watching me, thinking thoughts about me, perhaps forming opinions about the way I looked or the way I dressed. I had no idea what they were thinking or who they were.

In class I found Mrs. Ferguson, looking very much herself, familiar and welcome. I watched her move at her desk and at the chalkboard before the school day started, and I was unable to detect any difference in her demeanor, though she must have felt the change as keenly as I did, especially in those first moments.

Black students had taken the seats at the front of the class, and white students clustered in the seats to the rear. I expect we had a bewildered air. Ursula and Rhonda had taken their seats among the black students, and they faced us, the white kids, with an air that was expectant and perhaps a bit exultant. So, from the beginning I could feel many of the energies that would shape the rest of my school years: the lines of color that were drawn in the classroom and on the buses, the feeling that integration was a victory of black people over white people, and the sensation of being in the minority.

ABOUT HALF THE white students from my old class had made the decision to attend the new Pollocksville Academy, but it was Marianne's absence that I felt most keenly. We had been talking through the summer by phone, still maintaining the make-believe that we were in contact with popular singers and television stars, that we were actually aliens with incredible mental powers, that we were more than lonely country children in a county where there was never much to do for people who did not hunt or fish, who were too young to drink and carouse. It would have been easy, one would think, to maintain a friendship that had taken place by phone in summer months anyway. But once we stopped sharing a classroom, a chill fell over our friendship, and we lost each other.

Most of us were thirteen by then, as I would be before the end of September, and most of us were agitated by the changes that had taken place over the summer. This was 1968, the turbulent year in which Martin Luther King, Jr., and Robert Kennedy were assassinated, in which racial tensions kindled into fire across the country, in which people protested the Vietnam War and brought down the curtain on the presidency of Lyndon Johnson. By this age I had begun to follow the news, to read newspapers more regularly, and to understand something of the world. I had watched both political parties' conventions on television, following Huntley and Brinkley and their crew for most of the day. I brought this change with me to the new school, too, a new awareness of the world.

Like me, some of the other students were following the presidential election. At moments when Mrs. Ferguson was absent from the classroom, the two halves of the room hurled taunts back and forth. We covered the various topics that we would use for the rest of the year to pinch and provoke one another. The white kids brought up George Wallace and Richard Nixon, states rights, and the like. The black kids responded with Black Power, the Black Panthers, soul, Malcolm X, and the coming of the revolution.

Violet, who was now my classmate again, exacted a certain degree of payback. "Slavery time is over," she said one morning, in response to some crack Harry Bell made about the good old days. "The black man don't have to bow down no more."

"That's all right," Harry answered. "When George Wallace is president, you'll find out."

"I'll find out what?"

"You just wait, you'll see," Harry said.

"You be the one to get a surprise when the people take over," said a girl named Evelyn Hall, in a quiet, steady voice.

"That's right," agreed Ursula. "It's a revolution coming, y'all."

I reflected that last year she had promised to put me on the list of white people who would be spared, and I wondered whether she had remembered.

At lunch, the white students all sat together at one table, barely filling it. We brought our lunches, in my case two bologna and cheese sandwiches on white bread, a touch of French's yellow mustard on the bread, wrapped in plastic, carried in a brown paper bag. All the white kids ate lunches brought from home, turning our noses up at the food prepared by the black workers in the school cafeteria.

This strikes me as odd as I think of it now, since white families in the South employed black cooks, and white people never showed any qualms about eating food prepared by black hands in a white kitchen. The fact that all the parents sent us to school that year with bag lunches for the first time indicates a level of discussion and agreement behind the scenes. At the time I had no reservations about it and rather liked the novelty, though the sameness of the fare was wearing. Once or twice it occurred to me that the cafeteria workers might be insulted by the implications of our boycott of their food. I am certain this was something the black students noticed about us. Neither Rhonda nor Ursula had ever hesitated to eat the cooking at the white school during the years of Freedom of Choice. But this choice of ours was never a subject of much discussion beyond the in-class taunting that continued through the year. I expect the black students were not surprised by our behavior.

The white students drew closer together in the atmosphere of this new school, mostly because we were outnumbered and viewed with suspicion by the black kids. Knowing that enormous pressure had been brought to bear to force integrated schools on Jones County, the black students were skeptical of our attitudes. This does not mean we white kids liked each other any better, and I grew neither closer to nor more distant from any of my tablemates at lunch. But I felt the presence of the black kids in the lunchroom around us, as the days and weeks passed, and their faces and names became more familiar to me. I understood that our table of white kids represented a kind of stubbornness that I might have to face, a part of myself that I might come to question.

I HAD BECOME conscious of the wider world through watching the news, reading newspapers and newsmagazines, and especially through watching the election of the president in that fall of 1968. Like many other people, I felt as though I had a personal attachment to my leaders, and the fact that I would someday be a voter encouraged me to choose sides. This occurred after the assassinations of King and Kennedy in the summer, and after the conventions of the two parties, which gave me a sense of right and wrong where politics were concerned. I felt a kinship with Democrats and a distrust of Republicans. On the whole I liked television reporters and thought they were telling me the truth.

In Mr. Wexler's civics class, we discussed some of these topics openly. Mr. Wexler was also the principal, supervising the teachers and running the school. He was a black man in his late thirties or early forties, handsome if a bit plump, affable and smiling. He was my first black teacher and the first person with whom I debated issues of politics. We studied history and government with him, and our time in his classroom turned into a long discussion of the election, at least through the fall. He had a way of making discussion safe. He was a Nixon advocate, while I backed Hubert Humphrey. The fact that, under his guidance, we were sitting in a classroom in the South, black and white students discussing who should be president, strikes me as more important than anything else taking place that year. This is not to say that the conversations were elevated or the arguments cogent. We did not open up the more dangerous topics for debate, and avoided much mention of our situation, of the fact that we were dealing with integration ourselves. We never discussed our own history, the long past of Jones County. But we were talking, in ways that moved past our divisions, at least to a degree.

The networks were discussing the notion of the Nixon Southern Strategy, playing on Southern fears of integration.

Maybe because at school I was part of a minority of students myself, this idea caused me to examine myself and my ideas about skin color for the first time. My thinking on the subject moved from unconscious to conscious in that year. The national debate taking place indicated that the idea of race was far more powerful than I had suspected, perhaps the most powerful of all the ideas acting on my world. It became clear that I had a choice to make.

In our discussions about politics in Mr. Wexler's class, the opposing roles that we took on by accident, his advocacy for Nixon and mine for Humphrey, made me think even harder about what I believed. For Mr. Wexler, the Southern strategy was less important than distrust of the Democrats, their Great Society, and their many programs for social intervention. He had the feeling the government was overreaching. He was a middle-class man whose skin color appeared secondary to his worldview, a neutrality that he projected, no doubt by design, to make his classroom presence more appealing. He distrusted Humphrey because of his association with Johnson, and because of Vietnam. He also enjoyed the debate, and found me very amusing, I think. I was a smart child, and he liked smart students, as most teachers did. He also enjoyed the fact that now he was a teacher to all the children in the community, though he never said so directly.

There were many people whom I came to know that year, but the two who stood out, other than the friends I already had, were Evelyn Hall and Steven Rockley. Steven was the handsomest of the black boys, taller than me, solidly built, with skin of a creamy coffee brown. I found myself staring at him in class at times. Evelyn was a demure young woman with a rich, quiet voice. She had a strong, calm presence that resonated, and her manner of speaking was full of self-possession. She wasted no words.

We learned about each other, all of us, in those moments between our bickering, when we worked on a school project together, or when we talked about music, or television, or the news, idle moments at our desks, or moving from class to class. Some of this conversation sprang from simple curiosity. With the end of black and white separation, black people were curious about white people, and white people about black. But this curiosity took a backseat to other agendas. Sometimes when a black student spoke to me or asked me a question, I knew I was being tested. Some of the tests I failed. When asked about black musicians or singers, most of the time I was ignorant. I knew about the Supremes but not about the Temptations. I had listened to records by the Shirelles, an older group, but had no idea of the names of the singers.

"You know Malcolm X?" asked Violet one day, meeting my eye across the aisle, during one of these discussions at the end of a period change when we had moved from one classroom to another.

After a while, sheepishly, I shook my head.

"Malcolm X say the white man is a devil. You a devil. What you think about that?"

I shrugged. "I don't know."

"I believe white people killed Malcolm X," she said.

I did not know he was dead, and so I had no reply.

In spite of my ignorance, I was willing to talk. To an increasing degree, it was clear that many of my white classmates were not. Embattled and surrounded, they closed ranks, spoke disparagingly of James Brown and the Temptations, drew Confederate flags on their notebooks, and praised George Wallace, under whom, they claimed, the South would rise again.

One day matters came to a quiet peak. I was working with Evelyn Hall on a display for the bulletin board. We stood at the back of the classroom, lettering signs and cutting words out of construction paper. My white classmates were snickering and making some remark about what would happen once George Wallace was president. They were talking within their own group, but making a conspicuous show of it, a performance for the rest of the class. This was one of the moments when Mrs. Ferguson was absent from the classroom. Evelyn Hall turned to me and indicated the huddle of white boys laughing about the return of segregation. "You see your people, don't you?" she asked.

I said, "Those are not my people." I kept working quietly on the bulletin board. She took in my answer and said nothing more herself.

This was a defining moment for me, and even after so long a time has passed, I can feel my own calm as I said the words. I was making a choice.

I still brought my lunch to school every day. I still sat at the table with the white students. Breaking no conventions and behaving as was expected of me, I nevertheless had begun to stand apart from my white friends and to differ from their point of view. I accepted equality and its implications. No longer would I act on notions that my skin made me superior to anyone.

This, though, does not equate to erasing the ideas about skin color that were so deeply ingrained in me. I accepted equality but I still feared walking past groups of black boys, in particular, and I still dreaded confrontation with the anger of the black students, an anger I could see on their faces as they watched us in the classroom. I no longer acted on notions of my superiority but the idea that I was superior failed to disappear. (In truth, at that age, I thought I was superior to almost everybody, regardless of skin color.)

As for Steven, he tested me in a different way. I had been watching him a bit too much, I suppose, for he turned to me one afternoon, during our English class, and caught me staring. He asked, in a loud, clear voice, "Do you want to suck my dick?"

The question shocked me a bit, and the words hung over the classroom, everybody watching me. Time slowed for me, but I knew I had to respond with as little hesitation as I could manage.

I answered, "No, I don't." Knowing that I must not show any surprise, outrage, or fear, I spoke calmly and looked him in the eye. I have no memory of blushing but I suspect I did, a bit.

"Are you sure?" he asked.

"I'm sure," I said.

"Because you keep looking at me."

"Well, I still don't want to." I shrugged, and said nothing further.

What the other students made of the moment, I have no idea. There was no laughter that I recall, meaning, at least, that if there was it must have been minimal. I showed no embarrassment and, to my credit, I suppose, I felt none. Nor did I fear being exposed as a queer to the rest of the class. He might have an instinct that I was a sissy but he had no proof of what was inside me. I had never breathed a word of what was in my head. No one had anything on me. So I could face Steven down with only a moment of panic.

Still, I was more careful in the way that I looked at Steven after that, even when we became friends in later years.

His question let me know he had seen me clearly and that I had communicated my attraction to him, at least at some level. To the degree that it was possible for me to adjust my behavior, I expect I did. But I was resigned to my difference, and we were reaching an age when it would become more noticeable. The moment passed, though, never to be repeated.

I never connected my isolation from the other people, my queerness, with the change I underwent in the way I saw my black schoolmates. Only later would I understand the influence of the one on the other. I had never entirely accepted the social messages I received from my parents, my peers, and my surroundings, because I was different, and knew it. The white narrative of the world excluded people with desires like mine, and this prevented my believing that their ideas applied to me. I had already learned to see and think for myself in building my identity, even though I kept this part of myself silent and hidden.

Was I alone in the fact that my attitude toward skin color was changing? In this particular year I would have a hard time answering, and even for myself the path was muddied by exclusionary behaviors that I retained, including the bag lunches and the fact that in most ways I still kept faith with my whiteness. I never sat at a lunch table with the black students. I never attempted any close friendship across the color line. Even from Rhonda and Ursula I pulled back to a degree. But we kept our friendship through that transition, and I made other friends. The change I experienced was small and mostly hidden. Nevertheless, it was a real change, and it would last.

The Drowning

The Atlantic Coast Line Railroad ran through Pollocksville, crossing the Trent River on an iron railroad trestle on days when there was enough freight to justify the trip, which was most weekdays, often in the late afternoon. The rest of the time the trestle went unused, except for occasions when boys went swimming, diving into the murky water from the train tracks or from the higher platform some forty feet in the air.

The house my family bought stood beside the railroad tracks, next to the old depot and within sight of the trestle. This place would mark the last of our moves from house to house in the part of the county around Pollocksville. From our yard I grew accustomed to the occasional parade of boys headed to the trestle, and I watched swimmers in the distance, sometimes groups of white boys and sometimes black, never mixed. I had never learned to swim and thus never joined the groups.

My inability to resist watching the swimmers and divers likely added to the rumors about exactly what kind of sissy I was. Throughout these years I was aware that I was being called a sissy behind my back, though I paid it no mind. Since I was already separated from the other boys by the fact of my hemophilia, I had no reason to fear name-calling. I worried more about my weight than about any teasing I was getting. Except for my waistline my self image was fine, and I was a bit vain where my personality and mind were concerned. My sole worry was that I still carried what looked like baby fat. I had always been thin until I reached puberty, and then I bloated a bit.

Still, I watched boys swimming and diving and stared at their naked skin, their hurtling bodies. My desire must have been plain.

One day I watched a small group of black boys head to the river, dressed in old blue jeans cut off just above the knee. By this time I recognized some of their faces from school, and that was the case this day. A young man a couple of years younger than me was heading to the river—Warren, someone I knew by sight but to whom I had never spoken. The swimmers, their bodies gleaming, headed to the trestle, laughing a bit, talking to one another. Nothing out of the ordinary in this, since on a hot day the trestle and the river drew a fair amount of traffic.

Some time passed, and I noticed people going to the river, adults, and soon I learned that the boy named Warren had dived into the river but had never surfaced. I expect he had been diving from the high span over the trestle, the most daring point from which to leap. This was the picture I had in my head.

Dragging the river yielded nothing.

This information seeped into our house over the early and mid-afternoon. People passing our house gave us the story, somber voiced, relieved to have someone to tell the news, since it was hard news, and there is something pleasing to people about sharing hard news. The dead boy was a person I knew, even if slightly, and his drowning made me sad, coming so unexpectedly on a summer's day.

Late in the day, maybe in the evening around six or so, with the sun low, a large group of black people walked from the back streets of Pollocksville together. They moved quietly, with an air of sorrow. I watched from the windows, inside the house, moving from window to window to keep up with them as they headed down the railroad tracks to the river.

I never knew exactly what group this was, but I expect a minister led them to the river to pray for Warren, to say goodbye together, maybe thirty people of all ages. I had never seen this happen before, a group marching down our street. They stayed at the river for a while and then returned.

I felt no urge to follow them, though there were a couple of classmates of mine in the group. But the death struck me and my family as if we had a personal connection to it, by virtue of living so close to the trestle. Someone had drowned close to our house. The memory of the crowd and their quiet procession to the riverside stayed with me, and I wondered whether white people would have said a similar farewell had one of their own been lost to the river. Or would they have stayed in the house to watch, as I had done, letting the dead vanish without a good-bye? I had begun to see differently through the lens of skin color now. I questioned difference instead of embracing it. I had begun to think of white people as "they" rather than "we."

Warren had dived into the river but became entangled in the weeds. I learned this after the river was dragged without success, after divers were called in to find his body. The image was eerie, his body floating in the murk, trapped by some plant that would have looked so harmless if it had not ensnared him and taken his life. His death brought an end to swimming in the river there at the trestle.

Robert

O ver the years I had nourished a secret affection for Robert Andrews, the sandy-haired, husky, deep-voiced older boy who had failed fifth grade and thus become part of my class when I was still a student at Alex H. White. He was the handsomest boy in school, maybe in the whole town. I came to care for him so deeply it was like an ache in my core, a throb that belonged to my whole body; such a longing that even decades later I can feel the echo.

I tutored him in math in seventh grade, not simply for a few minutes but for the better part of two days. Mrs. Ferguson had set us to work individually while she circulated from desk to desk, correcting mistakes, explaining principles, and answering questions. She assigned me to help Robert, and so I moved a chair next to his desk and helped him work on his use of fractions. Sitting head to head with him, I explained how to add fractions, how to multiply them, and how to divide them.

While I would have counted many of my classmates as friends in those days, there were no boys with whom I was close. My hemophilia created a barrier between the world of boys, their rough play, and me, and by seventh grade I had become the sissy who had mostly girls and misfits for friends. This sounds meaner than it was; I endured hardly any teasing, and no bullying at all. But I never joined in games of softball or went on hunting trips, never joined the Boy Scouts, never went camping. So I knew little of the world that Robert knew. What he knew of me was all about my place in the classroom, the fact that I was supposed to be smart.

We worked on his math skills in earnest, doing the problems set out for us in the textbook, Mrs. Ferguson occasionally walking by to check on our progress. Sitting next to him filled my body with warmth that was pleasant and addictive, and talking with him felt easy. I liked the sound of his mellow voice. He understood the arithmetic well enough when I explained it to him, but a few minutes later he might or might not remember the rules I had taught him. Numbers on paper had little or nothing to do with the world he cared about, and he never retained much of what I tried to help him learn.

Some days later he stopped by my desk to whisper that Mrs. Ferguson had decided to give him a social promotion to eighth grade. He spoke very close to my ear, that voice reaching all through me. It was a secret, he said, so I shouldn't tell anybody. But he wanted me to know. I flushed with happiness that he had told me a secret.

This exchange made us friends of a kind, though not of a sort to hang out together or play together. This might have been different but for the fact that, as always, I could not do the things other boys did. Still, when I was in class with Robert, I could feel that we had drawn closer in some way. This sense was particularly acute during the first few days of the school year at J. W. Willie. I claimed the desk in front of his in class, and we talked a good deal.

On the first day there, with some obvious discomfort, looking at the unfamiliar faces in the class, he had said to me, "This is some mess, ain't it?"

"Everybody's in private school," I said.

He nodded. But it was clear that was not what he meant. "Jimmy, I'm going to get myself in trouble if I ain't careful."

He meant he would get into fights with the black boys. I could see the thought in his face. I don't remember giving him any response to that. But we talked about some of the other kids, like Anna, his cousin, who had been in class with us since first grade. He spoke as if he missed having her here, when I would never have guessed he had such a feeling. I expect he missed the old school, the old way, and that was the reason for his unease and anxiety.

Still, when he said my name I felt a change inside me, entirely unrelated to the new school or the new circumstances.

We were closer during those days than we would ever be again, save for one brief interval in junior high school. Mrs. Armstrong, our English teacher, took note of our friendship.

On the second or third afternoon of school, when she released the class for our afternoon physical education period, Robert asked to go to the water fountain, and she allowed it. I asked if I could go with him, and she gave us both a smile that acknowledged the sweetness of the two of us, and of my obvious hero worship. Robert saw this, too, and offered me his arm as we headed down the walkway. We walked arm in arm into the center of the school building. This was not characteristic of how boys behaved together in Jones County. Something was clearly afoot.

There were a number of black students near the water fountain, and they grew quiet and watched us as we approached. Robert dropped my arm and stepped to the water fountain, took his drink and made room for me to do the same. The simple fact of the two of us in the midst of the black students brought about a tension that I could feel. The black boys offered some kind of challenge to Robert, without saying a word. This was so early in the year, the change so fresh, that we were very uncomfortable with each other, still strangers, black and white. But I could see at that moment the difference in the way boys challenged each other, the threat that there would be a word that sparked a fight.

The next day, Robert told me his parents had decided to send him to the Pollocksville Academy, to the same class as Anna and my other friends. My heart sank, and the tide of joy I had felt began to ebb.

I missed him terribly. Once or twice I called him after school and we talked. I was shy of calling him because my feelings about him had continued to run so deep. We talked for a long time, and it was clear he liked the fact that I liked him, whether or not he understood what it meant.

When he reached junior high school Robert returned to public school, though by then he had a girlfriend, and drove his own car. We had only one class together, PE, during which I sat on the bleachers in the gym or on the football field and watched the other boys play. Our worlds only barely intersected. We spoke sometimes after lunch, or during class changes, but still there was some friendship between us, not entirely ordinary. He joined the junior varsity football team, one of a handful of white boys. One day, before a pep rally, he asked me to wear his jacket and take it home with me. I sat in the bleachers looking at him on the football field, the coat wrapped around me, people staring.

One day in gym class I was watching him with those feelings inside me. He was bounding around a small lobby at the side of the gymnasium, the locker-room door open; he was half dressed, coming very close to me and then backing away, bounding along the bleachers and then heading back to where I was. I could hardly believe that he was acting this way. He must have felt how much I wanted him. He took my hand and pressed it against his crotch. I drew back my hand right away, and said, "You really want me to do something, don't you?" I spoke without thinking, and afterward, neither of us could look the other in the eye.

"If you're crazy enough to do it, I'm crazy enough to let you."

There were a couple of other boys nearby. I thought he was making fun of me.

The whole cycle repeated; he pressed my hand against his crotch, and I said, "You really do want me to."

He repeated his phrase, too.

There was something charged in this moment, and it contained some part of what I wished. He had some understanding of why I watched him, and what I wanted from him. I had only to be crazy enough to take the step, as he said. He would allow something to happen, he said. I would have given anything to have something happen between us, but, at the same time, I thought he might be making fun of me.

I was afraid. He had no way of expressing tenderness, and was a creature of immediate appetites. No one had to tell me that I should be careful; so far, I had given no one any evidence that I was homosexual, and I had no intention of doing so. This was a decision that ran too deep for words, and even a hint of opportunity left me paralyzed. I felt a dread of what might happen if I should give anyone evidence of what I was.

But I wondered about the silent system within me that created this fear, the understanding that my caring for another boy would be dangerous if I carried my longing from wish to action. How much did it share with that other quiet set of rules, the ones that had taught me I was white and must separate myself from darkness? In coming to know black people for myself, outside what I was expected to see, how much did I learn about myself?

When the revolution came, would it also free me?

No Longer Separate, Not Really Equal

During my ninth-grade year, my civics teacher, a black woman named Mrs. Murphy, provided me a model of the classic schoolteacher, in manner reserved and stern, affable enough to be liked by her students, but not one to allow any sort of disrespect. She taught us the workings of our federal and state government, including a reading of the Constitution, the Bill of Rights, and the Amendments to the Constitution.

She was a tall woman, erect and slim, with a tidy figure. I recall her strong posture, her calm way of sitting at the desk or standing in front of the chalkboard as she lectured. She wore simple dresses, whites or pastels, modestly cut, skirts occasionally narrow but not tight, flat shoes, a set of wedding rings on her hands. She had an easy, friendly smile. If she had any sense of unease in teaching a room partly constituted of white children, some of them inwardly hostile to her, she never showed it.

Mrs. Murphy endured the change in school systems without showing much of the effort and anxiety it must have cost her. She had not been asked to teach at the high school and remained in the junior high school for the remaining years that I was in school in Jones County. If this caused her any disappointment, she left it outside the classroom. Inside, she was sure of herself, and I developed an affection for her over the course of the ninth-grade school year. This feeling of friendship with an elder led me to one of the acts from those days that showed how little I had understood, in a conscious way, about my bias against black people. For I thought I respected Mrs. Murphy as a teacher and a person.

One day in spring I found out that her first name was Betty, Betty Murphy. Knowing this name for some reason awakened in me a glint of mischief or daring, and at the end of a class period, I walked up to her desk and smiled and said, "Hey, Betty."

Her affable expression changed, her eyes sharpened, her brows knit together, and she said, "Jimmy Grimsley, don't you ever call me by my first name again. You will call me Mrs. Murphy. Do you understand?" She waited, her eyes fixed and insistent, while my stomach churned.

My little idea of a joke had earned me a moment of mortification. "Yes, ma'am," I said.

"That will be all." She pursed her lips, adjusted her glasses, and was done, and ignored me after that.

She had restored the authority required by the relationship of teacher and student. She had put me in my place, undercutting my attempt to demean her by use of her first name. I had tried to shame her, and she had told me she would not allow it.

The moment echoed. As I considered it, I realized that I had shown her a deep level of disrespect. When I called her "Betty," I had placed myself on an equal level with her, although I was a child and she an adult, I a student and she a teacher. With her admonition in my ears, with the sudden fear that she would not like me anymore, I was already blushing in embarrassment by the time I left the classroom.

The next day I apologized for having used her first name. I cannot remember the words I used. I hope I told her that I had not meant to disrespect her, though, if I did say that, I am not certain I was telling the truth. It would be more accurate to say that I did not understand the lack of respect until I heard the words come out of my mouth. And then I realized I must have intended it at some level.

She took the apology as her due and forgave me with a quiet, prim expression on her face. The apology satisfied her, but I doubt she forgot what I had done. I had crossed a line.

As for me, I learned that some part of me would test the black people around me, would bully them, would disrespect them, unless I took hold of it in some way. I learned that this behavior could take the form of an impulse that I would not fully understand until I acted on it. I was a functioning young bigot, a sneaky one, who might act only occasionally from this side of myself, but who nevertheless had the impulse.

Before, black people had simply been irrelevant in my world. Now that I was learning to see them as people, the prejudice I had learned moved to another place, acting with different tactics. The child sees difference, marks it; the adult acts on it. I would either learn to be a better bigot, or I would learn to stop being a bigot at all. Two paths. I had a choice to make.

I HAD ENTERED the ninth grade and attended what was now called Jones Junior High School. In that year, integration of Jones County schools was complete through all twelve grades, ending many decades in which our underfunded county operated separate school systems for the two races. If integration meant an end to racism, through the fact that the two races would now have to deal with each other directly, as equals, then that process should have been well under way.

But by then the county had already resegregated. The dual school system had reinvented itself through the actions of the private sector. Miserly white Jones County families somehow scraped together the resources to fund academies for the education of their children, designed to protect them from associating with black children, obedient to the idea that God never intended whites and blacks to mix. As if God had time to intend as many things as people claimed He did. Some of these private schools were operated by churches, and some were not. The Pollocksville Academy was now housed in a brand-new building outside town, about halfway to Maysville. I had started to forget which of my old schoolmates went there, since I no longer saw them. Now they were the ones who were invisible.

The junior high school building had formerly served grades nine through twelve for black students, and was located just outside the city limits of Trenton, the county seat. The white and black high schools had always had the same core programs, but overall there were some differences, most notably that the black high school had a substantial facility dedicated to instruction in bricklaying, training that was missing at its white counterpart.

At the junior high school, most of my teachers were white. I had homeroom with Mrs. Corbin, science with Mrs. Wells, civics with Mrs. Murphy, and language arts with Miss Trundle. I took mechanical drawing with a white teacher whose name I can no longer recall. In the afternoon I sat through physical education with Mr. Spears, the school coach, as teacher. Four of these were white teachers, two black.

Mrs. Corbin taught with a crispness that struck me as more modern than Mrs. Murphy. Both were easy to talk to, but with Mrs. Corbin I worried that I was wasting her time, while with Mrs. Murphy I felt her patience. The difference carried over to their appearance, Mrs. Murphy wearing neat print dresses that fit her well, but obscured her slight figure, and Mrs. Corbin, who was made along more generous lines, wearing clothes that hugged her body a bit tighter. Our white English teacher, Miss Ford, came to us directly from college, a stocky woman with short, dark hair and a fine, thin mustache. Mrs. Wells was likely the oldest of the group, her skin finely wrinkled, chin puffy and starting to form a waddle. For her, I dissected an earthworm, opening its pickled skin and pinning it to reveal the tiny, shriveled innards.

In junior high school I met children from unfamiliar parts of the county, from Trenton, Comfort, and Maysville. At the time, these strangers felt as exotic as if they'd sprung from different edges of a continent. The people of Jones County pretended that people from different parts of the county were vastly different from one another. The Pollocksville kids claimed the Trenton kids were stuck up. The Pollocksville and Trenton kids considered the Maysville kids to be hicks, and also stuck up. People in Comfort thought they were the best of everything. The need to imagine differences based on county geography had a long history in all the townships. We used these claims to reinforce our own groups, and to declare loyalty to our own place.

School was school, and students were students, and that year felt ordinary in many ways. As at any school, we were cliquish and petty, driven by gossip, secretly learning to drink liquor and smoke marijuana, clumped into social groups aligned in every sort of way. We noticed who sat next to whom, who liked whom, who should go ahead and drop dead, and the like, just as on any schoolyard. In the time between classes, it mattered that certain people walked together, and it was noticed, and the same general conversations occurred, about who was liked, who wasn't, who should suffer agony, and on and on. This felt familiar enough, an outgrowth of the habits of recess, though the scale was different, since there were so many students, compared to elementary school.

Looking back at that year I remember world turmoil, while school passed in a mostly tranquil way. Beyond our limited horizon, there were peace talks in Paris to end a war while bombs rained over North Vietnam. Charles Manson, using a madman's twisted logic, murdered people in California in order to bring on a race war, and the Weathermen tried to provoke another kind of war in Chicago. Black Panther leaders fought with one another. Woodstock happened. The president withdrew troops from Vietnam, and Jack Kerouac died.

In school, I learned about the Constitution of the United States, took mechanical drawing, rewrote Poe's "The Tell-Tale Heart" for an English assignment. Many new people crowded into view, and I grew fond of some. I watched Robert and his girlfriend and was jealous of her and felt longing for him. The novelty of integration had worn off, and we were simply going about the business of school. In some ways, skin color hardly mattered by this point. I had never attended a school of such size before and was most interested in the fact that junior high had so many people in it, every day. I was in a new world, larger than the little class at Alex H. White, or the slightly bigger one of the Willie school, and I took it in.

In most ways, we were still adjusting to the idea of housing all skin colors in one school. Once there, blacks and whites mixed only when necessary, and not in any settled pattern. The banter across classrooms often enough took on a scornful edge, one side preaching to the other; but our teachers never let this go very far. Within the school we invented a kind of separation, a habit of the races clumping rather than mixing. The result was only slightly more convoluted than normal for a junior high school.

The school itself, and the community behind it, made no effort to teach us how to see past our differences. Adults were silent on the subject of what it might mean to be black and white together, at least in public. In private, our parents quietly encouraged adherence to some version of the color line.

It would be easy to say, then, that integration was pointless, since segregation simply found a new pattern and reimposed itself at most levels. But we were in one place, in the presence of each other, no longer invisible. To be a white minority student in a majority black school system was teaching me all kinds of lessons. It was in fact turning the old world upside down.

Marianne came to public school for the ninth grade. But we had not talked by phone in months by then, and our friendship came back only to a degree. By then I had forgotten Davy Jones, and the game we had played in which we read the minds of pop stars seemed merely silly. She soon developed a crush on one of the boys who lived north of Trenton, and told me about him, a fellow who looked like Karl Green, the bass player from Herman's Hermits. Her attention was now fixed on boys in the real world. So was mine.

I shared classes with Rhonda and Ursula, along with the rest of the students on the college preparatory track. Most of the students in my class were white, even though most of the students in the school were black. I recall no discussions about that distinction in junior high school, though these subjects would arise again in later years. Rhonda and Ursula remained friendly, but they had their own social circle now, boys who thought they were cute and girls who wanted to be a bit like them. My friendship with them continued at a distance. Steven was part of the same track of students, and he shared some of the popularity spotlight. I stayed on speaking terms with most of the new friends I had made at the Willie School, but I grew closer to the college-bound students with whom I shared classes. I hardly saw Evelyn Hall any more.

We still spoke of two races only, black and white. I was trapped in this language, too, even though I knew that there were more skin colors, and had learned in biology that there was in fact only one human race. Skin color in biology was a minor matter of variation within a species, insignificant. In the world, though, its importance only grew as time went by. I understood some of the terms of the debate that was resonating everywhere, the aftermath of the Johnson years: the Great Society, the Voting Rights Act, fair housing laws, money spent to erase the wrongs of the past. But our public language was drifting beyond the notion of integration, which carried with it notions of assimilation that were no longer welcome. Black ghettoes across the country were exploding into violence, and the language of the revolution, the idea that black people would take power for themselves, would make their own world, had taken over the discussion. Race had become an issue that had siezed the nation.

Even at that age, I saw the irony in the fact that schools were no longer segregated at a time when Afro-Americans (a term used in that era) were discussing the formation of a separate black nation. But by then I would not have changed the schools back to what they had been before. My own life of hiding, of masking my sexuality and damping it down to nothing, would have been far harder in a white junior high school. In breaking the old social patterns, integration had done me a service. I saw this truth and felt a bit lucky, though still was not so daring that I ever acted on any attraction I felt. But at least I was not forced to pretend to have a girlfriend, or to trick a girl into thinking I liked her.

When I remember that year at Jones Junior High School, I am struck that I was biding my time, and that the rest of the students were doing the same. The schools were peaceful that year, students got along with one another, and we shared the school without much more bickering or quarreling than one would expect. That we refused to mingle completely was not a surprise.

We lived in a world that had taken a radical step in a direction of which we were uncertain. Integration was only one part of the sum. People had landed a spaceship on the moon over the summer. The 1960s were ending with violence, protest, and cities on fire. Would there ever be a Great Society or would Vietnam engulf us? Might today be the start of mutually assured destruction and World War III? I was hardly ready to understand the news I saw on television in any fullness, but even the contours and outlines frightened me. The world might come to an end in the blink of an eye, before I ever had the chance to live in it. When I thought in these terms, I felt a sense that anything might unfold, that tomorrow might bring a new disaster, causing everything familiar to change again. But still I went to class, prepared for high school, hoped for college, and saw barely beyond that horizon.

Cheap

The bus ride to the junior high school began on Highway 17 at the house where my family was living at the time, in the part of the county known as Green Valley. The bus carried us nearly to the county line, to the farm where my friend Dorothy Daniels lived, and then up 10 Mile Fork to the junior high school, a distance of over twelve miles, I would guess—a long ride at thirty-five miles per hour.

Bus drivers in North Carolina were drawn from the junior and senior class, teenagers with the proper license and the willingness to earn money by driving a bus route. These students were responsible for keeping discipline on the bus, for turning in students who were rowdy, started fights, or quarreled with the bus driver. At one time, I expect student drivers had been common to many states, but in 1969, North Carolina was the only place left that continued the practice, and the state would give it up a few years later. So the responsibility for keeping order on the newly integrated bus routes fell to students of one race or another.

Integrated busing had quickly settled into a pattern of turf, and on the bus routes I rode, the black students took the seats at the front and the white students the ones at the back. On the first days of our bus rides, Alex Burbank stood in the aisle and explained that the days when black people had to sit in the back of the bus were over. "Power to the people, right on," he said. He had a swaggering walk, and a rapid, almost clipped way of speaking. He was a natural clown whom I had known at the Willie School in eighth grade, though when I was the butt of his jokes I hardly found him to be funny at all.

We white students looked at one another and blinked. Since we were in the minority, it behooved us to accept the situation quietly, and we did.

Thereafter we followed a protocol of coexistence on our bus, one that never varied from day to day. White people filled the seats from the back, blacks from front, and the two parties negotiated the middle. White people and black people did not share seats, or make any attempt to do so. A certain amount of conversation was allowed across the hinterland, and some of the most raucous of the crossracial conversations took place here, especially at the end of the day when we were all heading home.

Within these broader guidelines, we maintained the usual

kinds of bus behavior learned in the long-ago of elementary school. Couples always had priority when sitting together, and they sat side by side holding hands, boy and girl, a look of silly light on their faces. Couples possessed the ability to sit in a transparent shell separate from the other riders, especially when they leaned their heads close to each other. No kissing was allowed on the bus, of course, but the couples managed to look fiercely intimate anyway.

The most desirable seats were those all the way in back, next to the emergency exit, with windows behind the seat through which one could make rude faces at the cars on the highway. Students raced to claim those. The seats at the front were equally coveted, since from those spots one could gaze in mockery or disdain at those who were struggling through the door and up the steps.

A white latecomer, either in the morning or afternoon, had to walk a gauntlet of black students in order to reach a seat. This served as a steady reminder that the black students refused to go anywhere near the back of the bus. When somebody from the front of the bus reminded us of this fact, as often as not one of the white students would reply that he or she liked the back of the bus better anyway. Maybe this was true, maybe not. It was a sensible assertion.

White people wanted to associate with white people, and black people wanted to associate with black people. This was a piece of what I had been taught. This notion found substance on our bus rides, when the color line descended in the middle of our bus, firm and immoveable, because we ourselves put it there. We reinvented it twice a day, on the trip to school and on the trip home.

In our part of the world, there was no discussion about school busing as a hardship; in Jones County, where there was only one junior high school and one high school, every student who was of age had to ride the bus for a half an hour or so. I was lucky on the bus routes that took me to school, because the Pollocksville kids in general left each other in peace. On some bus routes, black students filled up all the seats and refused to let white students sit down. This bullying behavior was more likely to take place when a bus was strongly dominated by one color or the other; I've heard from at least one student, not in Jones County, who rode on a bus where white students dominated and refused to let black students share seats.

Black students played a game among themselves, a verbal sparring, and when one person scored a particularly insulting comment on another, the victim of the insult was said to be "cheap." The hurler of the insult had to wait for reaction, either for signs of embarrassment in his or her adversary, or for someone in the audience to say, "He cheap. He cheap now, look at him."

Alex Burbank was a master of the game and, on the bus, would pace the aisle like a lawyer, speaking to one person or another. "Cassandra," he would say, "even your mama can't love you, because you got a face like a hatchet, you know what I'm saying, you look like a ax blade hit you in the face, you know what I'm saying?" He would keep talking until he scored a hit. "She cheap now," somebody would say, speaking of Cassandra, who might or might not have tried to fight back a bit. Sometimes he might attempt a rhyme or a kind of rhythm, but at other times he would simply start to speak, words rolling out of his mouth, so that I would wonder how he could keep talking so fast for so long.

To be cheap was to be put in one's place, rendered speechless, left without anything to say in rejoinder. One could prove oneself cheap simply by waiting too long to answer one insult with another, or by looking befuddled, or by being caught out in some kind of falsehood. When a person was found to be cheap, the whole community laughed at the sight. This was not a game white people had ever played before desegregation, but it was one with which we became familiar afterward. The bus rides were a good place to be made cheap, by engaging the wrong person in a debate and failing to trade insult for insult at the proper speed.

To get angry as the result of an insult was beyond cheap, entering the realm of aggression, the great sea of anger. To become angry was to lose the game.

The Mighty Trojans

I can remember walking up to Mercy and her friend Barbara one day in high school, the two of them tall and thin, long blonde hair all curl and frizz, dressed in faded jeans and army jackets, boots, leaning against one of the poles that held up the awning over the walkway. No one had thought to landscape the high school courtyard, and the grass was a wan, midwinter green, likely starved for a feeding. Andy Norton was standing with the two girls, dressed in more or less the same outfit as they were. He was one of the handsomest guys in school, a member of the football team, soon to be president of the student body, dark-skinned, with a smile that blazed. That was the day I saw that he was sweet on Mercy, and that she was sweet on him.

When I think of high school, I think of that courtyard, sunlight blaring onto the grass, the world all flat earth, open sky, and the school in some way naked under it. Neither tree nor shrub anywhere near, the school building sprawled in a field, two wings of classrooms facing each other across this bleak little open space, walkways running along it, another strip of classrooms running perpendicular to the courtyard. There was an actual hallway in that part of the building, leading past laboratories and home economics classrooms to the cafeteria and gym. Behind the main building, neat wooden walkways fanned in three directions, strings of mobile classrooms making that part of the school a bit like a trailer park.

Mercy had a sharp tongue, as I had learned, for instance, when, trying to be funny, I remarked that I was my own church, and she answered, without a missing a beat, "I guess it's a church of one." No one had to tell me I was cheap that time, though it's likely that someone did anyway.

Barbara and Mercy together defined a certain kind of hippie coolness that brought some feeling of the 1960s to the school. So did Lamar Vickers and his one-foot Afro hairdo, swaying from side to side in the breeze as he strutted from one class to the next. So did Stella Newman with her tiny waist and generous bottom, her sharp brown eyes, her tight blue jeans. We were an endless parade of flared blues, faded green fatigue jackets from the army surplus store, headbands, snug denim pants, and ankle boots.

Mercy and Andy had danced around each other for a while before everyone realized that they were starting to lean toward each other in that peculiar way. At first they simply talked, and then one day when Andy walked up to her, there was some change in their posture that happened at the same moment, almost as though they turned away from the rest of us, as if they separated themselves inside a bubble. We continued to talk as a group, likely some subset of the usual gang of us, but Mercy and Andy occupied some other space, beyond some transparent separation. They were now together in some fashion.

Watching this dance of theirs would form one of the most vivid parts of high school, for me. By the end of high school, Mercy would become for a while my closest friend, a change I would not have foreseen when I was a plump, redheaded sophomore, puffed up about my brain because it was all I had.

WHEN I ENROLLED in Jones Senior High School, I was part of the second tenth-grade class in the school's history. The old white high school had been called Jones Central, its colors red and white, its athletic teams the Rockets. As best I can recall, the old black high school had school colors of blue and gold; I never knew the name of the athletic teams there. When the new school was formed in the old building, students elected colors of blue and white, and selected Trojans as the name of our teams. Now, in the fall, as I became a student there, the high school football team was practicing, a handful of white players on the squad, and the mostly black cheerleading squad rehearsed its cheers. Such a small change in some ways, that this was simply the school responsible for the last three years of my education, and integration hardly mattered.

The feeling of high school was starkly different than anything that had come before. This was the end of the line. Seniors carried themselves with the strut of the oldest in the pack, almost finished with schoolrooms forever; the juniors were so close to the same milestone that they were giddy, too. We sophomores, the youngest class, waited expectantly for that same feeling to mantle us. All this was to be expected from any high school, I suppose. But this was a new school, only two years old. Simply in attending to our work here, we were doing something that had never been done before.

Some counties made a different choice, preserving schools, including school colors and mascots and closing historically black schools. By these actions, white people were seeking a bit of revenge for integration, or simply devaluing the black schools altogether. In taking another route, Jones County avoided some of the troubles that plagued her neighbors, where disputes and complaints about the closing of schools would continue for years.

Only a few dozen miles away, in Hyde County, Afro-Americans boycotted the school system for a year in order to put a halt to the plan to close all the facilities that had served them. Schools into which the black community had poured effort and struggle were to be closed in favor of white high schools, white athletic traditions, white school colors. The county would expand the old white schools at considerable expense, meanwhile closing down perfectly good facilities that were identified with black people. Hyde County protesters won their fight after two years. At the time, I never heard a single word about this action, even though I lived within an hour's drive of the place; I learned of it much later in life, when I began to read the history of my region.

Having absorbed the changes of desegregation, the Jones County school system set about returning to normal. The football team had already played for one season, and now it was time for a second to begin. Friday-night football games at the high schools must have played an important part in the past, though I had been unaware of them. But as a sophomore I started to attend, often helping out in the concession booth, selling soft drinks and popcorn. I paid attention to the football game and cared when my team won or lost. We did a bit of both that year. Televised sports were integrated by that time, and white fans were growing accustomed to cheering for black players, and perhaps this speeded the transformation.

Even though there were only a few white boys who were willing to play on the team with black boys, white students and some of their parents came to the football games, maybe because the games had been a tradition, or maybe because there was nothing else to do. The result was something not coerced, a mixing of black and white on Friday nights in the bleachers, an event people attended voluntarily, resulting in an intregrated social activity that was, most likely, the first of its kind in Jones County.

Eben Strahan starred as the running back for the Trojans, and he became a local football hero over the course of that fall. He was a regular fellow in the way of personality, easygoing, making friends across the color line. White people who rarely said much to the other black students spoke to Eben as if he were a friend, a sign that he had a leader's personality. He came from a good, old family in the county. He had his sights set on playing college football, and everybody said he had the skill and the talent.

The football game drew a crowd for a lot of reasons, among them that the game was a natural gathering place for the events that would take place afterward: driving around; drinking; finding other spots where different groups would meet, share their liquor, and spend the late evening in company with one another, finally heading off to the woods to park, make out, and maybe more. A date like that might have taken place mostly in Jones County, where the social offerings were very basic. Most couples interested in romance drove to Kinston or New Bern or Jacksonville when they wanted to hang out at a hamburger stand or watch a movie. The football game served a function that was too valuable to set aside simply because of race mixing, and so the tradition of attendance survived the consolidation of the two school systems.

This proved that the humans thereabouts were, in fact,

willing to mingle when there was a purpose to it, and when there was a possibility to maintain boundaries. One might almost have been encouraged by this development, see this as an important step forward. But off in the dark somewhere were the families of the white people who were not willing to take any such step, the ones who had built new schools for their children, the ones who would not be sullied by contact with black skin.

As if a curtain had lifted on the new act of a play, suddenly I had friends in the tenth grade, people whom I had known in junior high school, who came to matter more to me now. The previous several years of school changes had detached me from the group of children I had known in Pollocksville, many of whom were no longer in public schools anyway. At Jones Senior I felt most at home among the students in the college prep classes. These, as before, were made up of roughly equal parts white and black students, though any particular class could range one way or the other. Rhonda and Ursula became my friends again, not just people I knew; Stella Newman and Craig Everley became friends and rival students; Mercy Wheeler and Barbara Carter allowed me to linger in their aura of cool. We, along with a few others, formed a group of people who mixed the races in terms of friendships, conversations, friendliness, respect. We thought of ourselves as right-thinking people, as young hippies, maybe as nonconformists, in the language of the day.

People had hardened in their opinions and were making their feelings plain after two years of integration. White people were in general unyielding in refusing to mix with blacks in social ways, since this would have implied equality. While both races attended events like football, interaction among blacks and whites at the game was minimal. People might speak to each other, meaning, in Southern parlance, to say hello or good day or make some ordinary talk about the weather, the tobacco, crops in general. But whenever a white person was too friendly to a black person, the moment was noted, and comment was made. During the days at school, the races clumped and self-segregated in most social situations, including in the cafeteria, at assemblies, and in the many interludes when students changed class. Many white students never spoke to black students during the day, or had only the most cursory conversations. Interactions when they occurred were often strained by a fake friendliness. Actual hostility was rare, however; the parties that might have clashed or confronted each other instead kept their distance.

The idea of segregation had been adapted to circumstance, and the limits of acceptable behavior had changed for those of us who attended public school. Whites were to hang out with whites. We could be polite to blacks but this had to stop well before the line of friendliness. The mixing of the races could occur only at school or school functions, and even there whites had to stick together, preferring their own. A white person who mixed with blacks after school or on weekends was going too far. We were to make it clear that we had accepted segregation as a fact but would not be pushed beyond that. The protocol had begun to evolve at junior high, and the pattern carried over to the high school, where it solidified further.

This was what was expected. Like my close friends, I no longer behaved as expected and made friends as I pleased. But simply having friends who were black was no cure for years of training in bias.

I can remember walking from one end of the school courtyard to the other, at a time when I had made it clear that I didn't particularly care what white people thought of me anymore. I passed clusters of people I knew. Stella Newman said something funny and slapped at me with a composition book. This would be one of the moments when I saw Mercy and Barbara ambling together in the sunshine, and sometimes Andy might be at Mercy's elbow. Across the courtyard clusters of white students stood in the grass. By then nearly all the guys had long hair and the girls wore secondhand army jackets. They were watching me and my friends, who were mingling, black and white. I headed toward my next class, farther down the courtyard, passing sullen clumps of black boys and white boys, standing separately, slouching in nearly the same manner. None of them were my friends, though there were faces I knew. On the walk, I had the feeling I was running a gauntlet of eyes.

The faculty was mostly white. This imbalance would cause

problems before the year was out. In my three years in the high school, I had only one black teacher, and she was fired in the middle of the spring semester. That woman, Mrs. Blount, appeared to have some kind of collapse during the year, at first making erratic efforts at having class, then sitting at her desk and abandoning any pretense of a lesson, then simply not showing up at school anymore. I remember her more vividly than some of the more placid, more serviceable teachers. She had a fussy way of gesturing with her hands, and when she spoke French, she tilted her nose up just so. Whenever she spoke to me I had the feeling that she was looking at someone else, or at the wall behind me. She was finally let go and our new French teacher was a man, Mr. Sisk, a recent graduate of college doing his years of teaching to repay an obligation. He was very handsome and I became instantly enamored of him, and would remain so for his two years at the school. Alas, however, I did not learn any more French than before.

No one protested Mrs. Blount's firing, though a year later, when the school system tried to fire another black teacher, black students would walk out of class in protest.

While in the past the school had relied on stable teachers who lived in the nearby towns, following integration some of the older teachers retired, and the replacements were young people, many of them fulfilling a college-scholarship requirement or married to a soldier posted nearby on a military base. Vietnam had filled the army and marine bases with young wives looking for work, and these teachers had no knowledge of the county or its people. They brought strong young energy to their teaching, but they were white women, every one that I can remember.

I often felt tested by the people I knew, every action scrutinized. This was no different for me than it was for most other students, and for the teachers, too. The white students were watching to see who was too friendly to black people. Whites had been reinforced in their negative feelings about desegregation by the backlash against it in the South, typified by George Wallace's ongoing third-party presidential campaign. For many Southerners this caused a resurgence in Civil War nostalgia, with the Confederate battle flag reappearing as a symbol of defiance. Students drew it on their notebooks or placed bumper stickers with its image on their trucks.

Black students decorated their notebooks with the single raised fist of the Black Power movement and bumped fists when they greeted each other, but, for the most part, owned no trucks on which to place bumper stickers. They tested white students who wanted to ignore them, saying hello, forcing interaction, in order to gauge how freely response was offered. This had been going on since the early days of integration, but in high school I noticed it more. "Why you don't speak?" a black student would ask of a white person. "You don't want to speak to me, do you?" To which a blushing white person might offer some fumbling answer about not paying attention, didn't hear you, didn't see you there, or the like. Or offer a weak, "Oh, hey." Others of us simply said hello, made eye contact, and moved on. Individual interactions between the races were still bound by the laws of politeness, and even a white person with a Confederate battle flag drawn on her notebook would attempt to be polite in the face of a suspicious Afro-American. This was politeness with a purpose, as Southern courtesy has always been. To have replied in any discourteous way would have invited escalation and perhaps conflict. White students were sullen but wanted no violence. We were outnumbered, after all.

I am hesitant as to where to place myself in all this. I was still a racist by training but I had abandoned as much of its practice as I could find in myself. Lacking the self-awareness to compass the process going on inside me, I was cautious in all my dealings. The day-to-day workings of my consciousness contained all the old elements of white supremacy, but alongside these were the mechanisms of the other knowledge I had gained. I was aided in this by my friends, the white and black kids who mixed, who made friends with each other, who talked.

White and black interactions were constant, and ran the spectrum from surliness to occasional courtesy to outright liking and open affection. High school opens up all these emotions in any case, but in our case, we had the added layer that we were the first classes in which the two races mixed. It was not simply a matter of a group of students who had mixed friendships while the rest snarled at each other; relationships of all kinds and flavors took place, all at once, without rehearsal. We behaved toward each other in all possible ways except with open violence. The adjustment, learning to live together in one school building, took place very quickly, and a sense of normalcy followed. Though always there was tension, the flaring up of disputes and confrontations, the usual sparring and spatting of teenagers with the added edge of race.

Certain sights always made me look twice, which indicated they touched my programming in some way. A black boy talking to a white girl always drew my attention, especially if they were alone, especially if no one was near them. This even though I had friends who were flirting, and perhaps more, across the color line; this even though I was aiding and abetting their romances. Still I would always look again to make sure of what I had seen. The same if a black couple were standing very close or kissing. I had to look twice. Movies and television were rife with images of white people spooning and groping and connecting in various ways. I saw people at high school who did the same, like Robert Andrews and Delores Rickets, or Eustace McKinney and Ellen Bell, and I thought little of it. But I had never seen black people in love with each other, holding hands, kissing, and, of course, that was what high school was all about for everybody.

Had I seen two boys mooning over each other in that high school courtyard, I would probably have dissolved from fright.

Was this reaction sprung from my prejudice, or was it simply a reaction to sights I had not seen before? The likely answer is that both causes played a part.

BUT IN THE case of Mercy and Andy, I never felt a sense of strangeness when I watched them together, maybe because I knew them both, or maybe because I only rarely saw them in some kind of physical contact with each other. At school they courted in a discreet way, hands shoved into pockets, looking but hardly touching, standing a bit closer to each other than to anybody else. As a couple, they radiated a sweetness that was palpable, both them of them too shy to show too much of their feeling, neither of them able to disguise how much they were attracted to each other.

Their coming together would play itself out against a background of national drama, and they would be the first interracial couple to be acknowledged at our school, though they themselves never made their relationship very public. We could not help but watch them, I suppose. People in love are often fascinating to watch.

Some of Us Dancing

The school hired a band to set up in the gym after football games, often the band for which Lamar was drummer, his hair shaking and keeping the beat as certainly as his hands and feet. Faculty chaperones stayed to keep order at these dances. The band played songs that everyone recognized, covers of soul hits, mostly. These dances provided another place for students in the county to gather, and the need for that trumped the need to segregate. Students of both races showed up at the dances, listened to the music, and experimented with this new social setting.

The first of these events took place after one of the early football games, and I attended with my friends. My sister Jackie and I had taught ourselves to dance on Saturday afternoons watching *American Bandstand,* and whatever money we earned from babysitting usually went to buying 45-rpm records. I never knew exactly what steps we were practicing, I simply moved the way I saw the dancers on television move. But she and I made the house shake, rather literally. She was a good dancer and so was I.

My church taught that dancing was of the devil, that Christians shunned such movements, but I had been dancing since I was small. The first named dance I remember doing, years before high school, was the Twist, listening to the Chubby Checker record while my parents were visiting a friend who had a stereo. Even at that age I liked moving to music, and so did my sister, so that our later dance rehearsals on Saturday afternoons felt familiar, and when we danced together we connected in a different way, an affirmation of one another. The house truly did protest a bit, and sometimes the knickknackery shook on the shelves. It was not a terribly substantial house but it did hold up under our hip-swiveling, gyrating, and two-stepping.

We danced to soul music, like nearly everybody else in the country. We danced to the Supremes, the Temptations, Sly and the Family Stone, Smokey Robinson and the Miracles, Marvin Gaye. We danced to the best beats on *American Bandstand.* It is odd that we accepted these black musical groups but, for some reason, like other white people, shied away from James Brown. Maybe his music was too raw and erotic, maybe we felt it was for black people only and not for us. His sexuality was open and he displayed it in performance, and this was likely too much for me at sixteen. We also danced to music by white groups, when it had a decent beat, but soul music offered a more reliable background sound for our groove.

After all that preparation, my sister and I had no intention of missing the school dance, and so, after the football game, we went into the gym to hear the band.

We were each with our friends, mind you. My sister was too cool to be seen with me at school, and I had my own friends, as strange as it seemed.

A number of the white kids showed up, too, maybe because there was nothing else to do on that particular (or most any) Friday night in Jones County. At first I sat in the bleachers with my white friends. There were a few dozen black couples on the dance floor, and the band was pretty good, Lamar was a strong drummer. The musicians had Afros the size of pumpkins. They played loud and hard. The dancers were, some of them, doing steps I had practiced with my sister.

As I recall it, Stella, one of my black friends, asked me to dance, and I knew it was a dare, another test, but I also knew I could do it, and so I stood up and danced with her, to a song like "The Tears of a Clown" or "Band of Gold." Maybe I danced with Jackie first, though, and we cut out a place for ourselves on the gymnasium floor, and maybe that was why Stella asked me to dance in the first place, because she already knew I could keep up. Anyway, we were dancing, a few mixed couples, a lot of black couples, while sullen white kids sat on the bleachers. The white guys were not asking anyone to dance at first, so my sister danced with a black guy. As she told the story, one of the local farmboys said to her afterward, "I'm really disappointed in you, Jackie. I thought you were a good girl."

She responded, "I'm just fine, Eustace," and moved on past him.

No one said anything to me.

The choice to dance and the choice not to dance were each cultural decisions, and both expressed long-standing differences. The fact that black people danced as a group celebration was one of the facets of character that the white world used to support our characterization of them as primitive. Afro-American culture found movement to be easy and natural, the rhythm of the body matched to music, to the drum, to the spirit, and this was visible in the way the black students of my school interacted. Even in the brief intervals between class periods, girls sometimes showed dance steps on the way from one room to another, and the guys demonstrated their jive walk. Whereas white children found movement to be suspect and possibly evil, born as we were among Christians who found in dancing a gateway to all the sins of the body. Disapproval of dancing was disappearing even before desegregation, but it had not yet vanished.

But nothing could keep dancing from looking like fun, like something that a person should enjoy. Nobody told me I shouldn't take part because of my hemophilia. So it was that I danced, uncertain Baptist that I was.

When I danced, I was simply moving to a beat that compelled me, not caring about any statement my body was making concerning equality or morality or the gatekeepers of sin. If there was a beat, I felt it; when other people were dancing I started to move, and I would dance with anybody who was willing to show me steps. As the music took over and the loud beat rattled through us, the dancing got easier, and the fact that we were simply having fun drew more and more people onto the dance floor. Even the white couples danced after a while, the boys giving it a try. So, like it or not, wrong or not, perfect or not, we had fun together, in spite of ourselves.

None of the white girls ever disapproved of my dancing, whoever my partner might be, since they were frustrated at how hard it was to get the white boys to dance. White boys were reluctant to move like that in front of their peers. Sometimes they would do it anyway, and as the season of dances progressed, it became easier to get white couples onto the dance floor. More mixed couples appeared. Indeed, once I became established as a willing dancer, both white and black girls kept me busy, and I hardly ever sat down during any of the dances that followed.

The strange, awkward dances of sophomore year evolved into the familiar, awkward dances of senior year, and by then a certain sense of normalcy had settled into our high school. The fact of desegregation had become established, we had grown accustomed to the sight of each other, knew each other's names. High schools were always and perhaps will always be full of factions, no matter the circumstances. Once we were no longer strangers to each other, we moved to the default level of high school pain, awkwardness, and discomfort that was and is the lot of teenagers.

A network of friendships formed among a solid core of black and white students, maybe forty or so. We were part of the college prep group, academic achievers; we were the group who were in the drama class, or Jones County's first creative writing class; we did the yearbook, and sat on the student council. We were the kids who hung out together on the smoking patio, including those, like me, who never smoked tobacco. At the dances we were the kids who danced together, and planned the dances, and decorated the gym. Our friendships made a matrix that drew the two parts of the student body into some form of a whole, even when its parts refused to associate with each other directly. We were the intersection.

I was only dancing, not dating, not loving, not marrying. I mixed freely with black people at school but none of my black friends called me at home or visited me there; but I suspect my hemophilia was to blame for this, since I know of other people who did visit each other. Such contacts as did occur outside of school were secret and hidden. One white friend of mine admitted to me that one of the black guys called her at home and they talked, but he pretended to be me, because he had a quiet voice like mine. This was the reason for her confession, I suppose, that the two of them had involved me in their deception. In this need to hide our friendships away from school, we children were following the lead of our parents, who had been forced to accept this much segregation but refused to give way to more. White people and black people remained separate in the larger life of the county, and their ideas of difference remained intact, ready to be transferred into their children.

I never danced with a boy in high school, or dated a boy, and the only one I kissed frightened me by proposing that we have sex the next day, in his house, while his parents were away. I broke off any contact with him and committed what was likely the worst sin of my childhood by telling my parents about him; I was agitated by the kiss and the idea of sex and could not sleep, finally confessing to my mother what the problem was. Nothing happened except my embarrassment at having told what should have been a secret, but it was a betrayal nonetheless. I did date two girls, once each, and then abandoned any attempt to take these relationships further, knowing that I would be no good at pretense. This was, in fact, the extent of my romantic experience in high school.

In an all-white high school, the fact that I was queer would have caused me problems, and likely I would have started to date a girl, pretending to love her in order to provide a cover for myself. But the fact that the social core of our school had been dismantled prevented the kinds of harassment I might have experienced otherwise. I was protected by my friends, who hardly cared that I was a bit effeminate. I was protected by the fact that I would dance with people, that I would talk and laugh with black girls the same as white girls. I was protected by my hemophilia, which had always kept me separate from the group of boys, and by the fact that I was smart and cool. In an all-white high school, the cool kids would have been defined differently, and I would have been nowhere near that group. In our high school, to the degree that the cool kids existed, I was one of them.

Dancing brought me out of myself into contact with these other beings from whom I held back so much, all the secrets I was keeping, all the things that I dared not share. In this I doubt I was much different from the other teenagers there. We all felt isolated, we all felt alone. But when I was dancing I understood that I was one of many, not so different, not really apart from the rest. When I turned out to be a decent dancer, I knew I had a place among those kids. I knew I would be all right.

The Human Relations Committee

One day early in my sophomore year, the principal, Mr. Cooper, asked me to serve on what he said was an important committee designed to provide a forum for discussions of problems related to integration. Flattered, I agreed to be a part of the group, and he told me when the first meeting would be held.

We assembled for that first meeting of the new Human Relations Committee in one of the school's temporary classrooms, mobile units that had been trucked to the back of the grounds and laid out in an L-shape around the new library and science classrooms. The name "mobile unit" glorified what was actually a double-wide trailer in which desks, chalkboards, and fluorescent lights had been installed. A couple of narrow windows brought in frames of the outside world, a view of the flat, brown football field.

Mr. Cooper was a slim, athletic fellow in his forties or early fifties, with the kind of aging good looks that made me guess he was a former athletic coach of some kind who had furthered his career by moving into administration. He had married a woman with a ready-made family; she was shy and a bit introverted, as I noted the few times I served as their babysitter. They made an odd group, since the three sons all looked like her, remarkably so, and Mr. Cooper hardly resembled any of them. They were like a family he had bought on discount, as an accessory.

At the first meeting, he opened proceedings by saying some appropriate things. We were gathered in this committee, he said, because we were the best and brightest students in the school, known for our level-headedness and academic achievement. He had chosen two students from each class, one black and one white, and we, along with Mr. Cooper and the vice-principal, Mr. Worrell, would consult with each other over issues that might come up between the races now that integration had come. I don't recall that teachers had any representation in this group at all. The school's administrators spoke for the school, and that was that.

We were a new school, Mr. Cooper stated, and we were starting over. We had chosen school colors that were different from the old white high school and the old black high school. Our sports teams wore new uniforms, and so did our band. This was a fresh beginning. We needed to learn to listen to each other, to get along, and to conduct ourselves like ladies and gentlemen. As such speeches go, it was a respectable effort.

The committee sounded like a good idea. We students looked at each other, knowing that we had all been chosen. We were very satisfied. Most of the chosen were boys, of course, but at the time I thought little about that.

The first issue Mr. Cooper presented to us was that of homecoming queen. Since the high school was nearly two-thirds black, an elected queen would nearly always be a black student. This might cause tension in school. Could we think of a different way to select homecoming queen that would be less of a popularity contest? We thought about it. We proposed that the selection of homecoming queen should be decided by fundraising. Each homeroom would select a candidate, and these candidates would compete for the crown by raising money for the school. This would be fair, we decided.

In practice, the decision would lead to homecoming courts that were mostly white, and white homecoming queens, at least for several years. Our decision ignored the fact that fund-raising was much easier for white students than for black students. During my years in school, this process caused no friction, but it was changed a few years later.

This decision revealed a good deal about what we presumed integration would look like. A majority black student body would never elect a white queen. The fact that black students were the majority and that they were entitled to cast their votes as they wished was unsettling to the committee. Had we been a white majority in the school, I suspect the notion that electing a homecoming queen was unfair to anyone would never have arisen.

The next important issue Mr. Cooper wanted us to discuss was the selection of a graduation speaker. He wondered whether we should continue with the practice of having the valedictorian speak at graduation, in light of the fact that white students were perceived to have academic advantages over black students. I do not recall his exact words, and would guess that he did not speak quite as plainly as I have done, since it was not his habit. Mr. Cooper was more affable than honest. Someone proposed that the graduation address be delivered by the student body president rather than the valedictorian. This would enable each class to have some voice in electing its own speaker.

On the surface, this decision offered a more open process, but it also presupposed that a black student was not likely to be valedictorian, an assumption that was faulty and biased. However, the notion that black students were not getting a fair chance in the classroom was one that would arise again and again. When our school finally formed a chapter of the National Beta Club, there were only a handful of black students in the group. As it turned out, the first several valedictorians of the school were white, in fact.

We had the discussion and came to these decisions, and the school operated under them for the next few years.

In other schools in eastern North Carolina, incidents related to homecoming courts, school colors, and band uniforms provided reasons for discord and even violence. Mr. Cooper was prudent to raise the questions, even if our decisions were flawed. Our school would suffer from discord in the coming two years, but not because of questions about the homecoming queen.

Once these decisions were made, the committee foundered a bit. While Mr. Cooper noted that we were starting over, that this was a brand-new school, he took the idea of dialogue no further than necessary. We scheduled no series of meetings, formed no process for seeking out grievances from students.

In the setting of the meeting itself, the principal and administrators talked, the students responded to questions, and the conversation remained fixed in a kind of hierarchical pattern. The issues to be debated were decided by the adults, and the correct answers were those to which the adults agreed. Since we were meeting in a bleak little classroom, fluorescent lights blaring and buzzing, tiny windows providing little relief against the heat, we were not disposed to linger.

Mr. Cooper had good intentions, perhaps, but little real sense of the problem that he faced in dealing with this student body. He was content when students behaved well, moving from class to class without fuss. The notion that there was a deeper layer of discord, one that could benefit from discussion and communication, was lost on him. He was content to read the surfaces. Soon enough he would learn that this approach was not enough.

I was clueless as well, and simply thought that it was nice that the teachers and principals had noticed me and selected me to be on this committee. This tickled my teenage vanity. I was trusted as part of a decision-making body that included adults. But in my case, I was young and stupid and could be expected not to see beyond the end of my nose. Adults should have known better, and I don't doubt that our teachers knew that there was more need for dialogue than our little Human Relations Committee could provide.

We left that first meeting feeling very pleased with ourselves. I can remember no other meeting of the group until after the black students of Jones Senior High School staged their first walk-out, later that year.

Protests

One morning in January, I was sitting in French class, waiting for another lesson from Mrs. Blount, the French teacher who would be fired in a few weeks. This was a Monday morning, and the room had a sleepy feeling as we waited for the bell. We had not quite resigned ourselves to the passing of the weekend. The room was a glare of white, from the fluorescent tube lights to the cardboard-thin walls and speckled linoleum. A couple of chalkboards sat forlornly on the walls, and at one end of the room was cabinetry and a countertop. This room was long and thin, a trailer but not a double-wide, and the shape of the room made it awkward for lectures.

There was no sign of class beginning, however, and Mrs. Blount simply waited at her desk. She was never an engaging teacher, and it was not unusual for her to begin class late. The tardy bell rang, a distant sound, drifting from the main building to our little room at the periphery, but I remember the ringing had an odd echo, and I was perplexed by it, since most of the seats in the classroom were empty. None of the black students had yet come to class.

Those of us who were present looked at one another. We were no longer quite comfortable sitting in a room with only white students, even those of us who did not much like integration. Something was afoot.

A latecomer arrived, bringing rumors about a demonstration in the hall leading to the teacher's lounge. This was Mitch, one of the student bus drivers, who had been delayed in making his morning report to the vice-principal. "It's some kind of riot in the hall," he said.

Hearing him, Mrs. Blount said, "What do you mean, a riot?"

"All the black kids is out in the hall," he said.

"Are they rioting?" asked Barbara.

"They're just standing around, I guess."

Mrs. Blount had sat up straight and adjusted her glasses. "Don't spread rumors, now. Let me see what I can found out." With this admonition she left the classroom in search of information. When she returned she told us that we were to remain inside the classroom, that classes would not be changing.

"There is a demonstration," she said. "In the main hallway."

"What's going on?" asked Faye Ollins.

"I just told you everything I know. There will be an announcement on the speaker, maybe." She folded her hands at her desk, then drew out her lunch from a brown bag and started to eat her sandwich.

Mercy, Barbara, and I conferred a bit. None of us had heard anything in homeroom, and, since we would have seen most of our friends for the first time in this French class, we had no idea what had happened or what was going on. "Do you really think there's something going on?" I asked.

"Must be," Mercy said. "Nobody's here."

"I wonder what it's about," Barbara said.

Mitch, who sat in the seat ahead of mine, was affecting superior knowledge due to his tardiness. "I seen 'em, they're all out in the hall doing something," he said. "Ain't this a mess?" Despite his words, his tone was more lackadaisical than outraged; even on the best day, French hardly felt like much of a class.

"If it gets me out of French class, it's fine with me," said Barbara. "I wanted to skip school today anyway."

"I bet they let us go home," said Faye Ollins, with a broad smile.

There followed a period of about an hour when we knew little or nothing other than that school was to be dismissed. We were understandably gleeful at the prospect and some of us thanked the black kids for being mad about whatever they were mad about. Others spoke as if this were an act of disorder that should be condemned. But nobody took that too seriously. These were years when there were demonstrations, walkouts, and outright riots even in the best places, and for many reasons.

People acted out about racism, about women's rights, about the war, about poverty. There was something exciting about the thought that we actually had civil disobedience in Jones County, too.

The bus ride from school to home was memorable, black students feeling the adrenaline of what they had done, energized by the statement they had made, white students cowed and silent. Alex Burbank strutted from seat to seat, saying, "That was some shit. Can you dig it?" From listening to the talk at the front of the bus, I could begin to piece together a narrative. The students were angry with the teachers. One of the teachers had said something. Black students had walked out of class, congregating in the main hall and the courtyard outside the shop class. Somebody threw something. Somebody got hurt. Accident. The students had been trashing the teachers' lounge and somebody threw a bottle.

Piece by piece, statement by statement, the story came out. They were in a kind of headspace I had never seen before, hyperalert, giving information in tones that did not invite much follow-up. "Power to the people, right on," said Alex Burbank, and heads nodded as if all were testifying. He spoke in a rhythm that I could hear but that was different from his usual voice, as if he were channeling someone else, and the response from his friends was united, almost eerily so, as if they were all joined minds. Maybe because they had been in a group action so recently, this was how they felt.

Tensions between the black students and the teachers, most of them white, had flared into violence upon reports that Mr. Taylor, one of the teachers in the vocational classes, remarked that blacks were the scum of the earth. Why he felt the need to make such a remark, when he did it, and who heard it—none of these details ever became clear. At the time I heard only that he had said something nasty about black people, but later read the quote as it was reported in the *Kinston Daily Free Press.*

The walkout and violence that followed responded to the remark in unequivocal terms. Black students surrounded the shop, filled the hallway outside the teachers' lounge, and destroyed a vending machine. Someone threw a few bricks through classroom windows, and students threw some of the soda bottles from the vending machines. One of the drink bottles struck a white student, Byron Johnson, though by accident, according to what I heard and to the newspaper report. His was the only injury.

Jones County, where little or nothing ever happened, had an event on its hands, a genuine insurrection. Black people were rioting right here where we lived. White people used that word for it right away, *riot,* and I did too, the same as everybody else, unthinking. The other names for it, *walkout* and *demonstration,* were never as popular, too tame and inadequate. Reports appeared in the local papers, the *Kinston Daily Free Press* and the *New Bern Sun Journal.* For a week our high school was the talk everywhere, but even so, there was little enough to say. A couple of windows had been broken, one vending machine was trashed. I even heard contradictory stories about the vending machine, some people saying it had merely been moved out of the teachers' lounge. Nevertheless we had an event to remember now, caused by integration. Other cities and towns had their riots, and now we had ours.

At home after school, my sister told me that one of her friends had given her a warning as soon as she got to school. "We like you," said the friend, a black girl. "But some stuff is about to happen. You on your own today."

The issue the students addressed was real. The Jones County school superintendent affirmed this when he was quoted in the Kinston paper as saying that the students were voicing a legitimate complaint. The issue was not limited to one teacher, though it was the words of the one teacher that sparked the conflagration. The white faculty had made it clear in all but words that they had little respect for black students, other than the gifted. Some of the teachers appeared bitter at having to serve in integrated classrooms. I could see this at the time, but had no clear way to understand the causes of the reaction.

For black students, the victory of integration had come with a cost. Most of the time, they were not in classrooms with black teachers who served as role models, as examples. Their teachers were no longer people of their own race, who saw them as human beings of equal status with all the rest. School was no longer a haven from prejudice but was rather a study in it.

Students in all-black classes now—and these classes continued to exist—were second-class citizens of their schools.

To give this picture some balance, I do not expect our teachers were excited about teaching white students in all cases, especially when they were less than gifted, or from the poorer parts of the county, or when the students showed their own apathy toward school, as so many did. The students in the vocational programs were moving toward trades that were often dominated by one race or the other. Classes there were resegregating along color lines—white people in the agricultural classes, because white people owned the land; black people in the bricklaying classes, because black people laid the bricks.

White adults reacted to the disturbance in the schools with mockery, especially those who had placed their own children in the new private schools. This was the kind of behavior you could expect from niggers, a remark I heard in church, offered as proof that the races should not be mixing in this way. The matter was debated in the local restaurant where my mother worked as a waitress, too. That place was owned by the Russell family, who sent their children to Pollocksville Academy and later to a school in Kinston. The Russells, like other private school families, appeared smug about their decision, satisfied with the fact that they could still find a way to keep their precious young from contact with Negroes. Though we went to church with the Russells, they no longer felt quite like neighbors.

The public high school was no longer really part of the white world, the local world, in the view of these people. The school was now marked out clearly as an arm of government. The government had sided with black people for good and all, and here in the riot was the result. The schools were "ruint," as Jones County people said.

The reaction on the part of black adults was probably as divided as the white adult response, with some glad about the walkout and others feeling that the students ought not to have carried the incident that far. But it is also likely that some black parents were part of the planning for the event at school, and that they encouraged their children to take action, and supported this choice.

Because I was a member of the Human Relations Committee, the principal called me to come to a meeting at school on the day after the demonstration. He had arranged a ride for me with another student who was also attending, since I had no car of my own. We met in the home-economics classroom, in which two fully outfitted kitchens occupied one wall, dusty venetian blinds at the windows, winter light settling over us. Mr. Cooper opened the meeting and thanked us for coming. He announced that schools would open again the following day and that he wanted to consult with this group about making sure the restarting of school went smoothly.

We discussed nothing in particular of importance, and I expect the meeting was intended to create a feeling of action rather than to achieve anything in particular. We discussed the issue of Mr. Taylor and whether he should apologize for the remarks he made that set off the demonstration. We talked about unlucky Byron getting struck in the head. We discussed the issue of whether the students involved in the violence should receive any kind of discipline. The principal planned to reactivate student government, which had been dormant since school consolidation, and to gather students to talk about this when school started again.

The walkout took place on Monday, the meeting of the Human Relations Committee on Tuesday. When classes resumed on Wednesday, the courtyard and public areas buzzed with talk of what had happened and what might follow. White students had less to say about the aftermath than one might have expected, given the talk I had heard in church and on the streets of quiet Pollocksville. I recall only a few mutterings, and no complaints at all about the missed day of school. Teachers for the most part remained mum about the demonstration, though some exuded disapproval and muttered a remark or two about the hopeless rudeness of young people.

Some conversation happened, in private, on the smoking patio, or during walks from class to class. In general, white students expressed mostly disapproval about the demonstration, even though most of them remained ignorant of its cause at this point. Black students obviously felt satisfaction that they had taken action and made their feelings known. Everyone agreed that the problem here was not between the students, and the school returned to its relatively peaceful norm. The shop instructor was dismissed from his job, or was allowed to resign, though, again, little or no word of this reached students in any official way.

We were left to trade rumors about the walkout and its causes, and the rumors soon established themselves as facts, even though they were false. Most white people never learned about the teacher or his remark about the scum of the earth, or else learned it but decided some other explanation would be more interesting. Years later I would hear white people repeat the story that the black students rioted in order to get out of classes for exam week. I would also hear that the problems at our high school were instigated by visitors from New Bern, where the high school had to be closed due to conflict the same day. But newspaper accounts of the New Bern school problems made it clear that the issue there was between students, while the Kinston newspaper confirmed my own memory, that the walkout in Jones County sprang from a hostile remark made by one of the white teachers.

Since the conflict had never been between the students, our pattern of behavior toward one another went unchanged. This is not to claim that our relations were in any way harmonious; they were simply never hostile to a point that approached group violence. But the underlying problem remained, and black students continued to feel conflict with the teachers and administration. These problems would arise again the following year.

IN FEBRUARY OF my junior year, the principal moved to dismiss a black math teacher, Mr. Fleming. In the aftermath of this action, black students walked out of class once again.

My memories of this second year of protest are more sketchy than those of the first, though the event proved to be more prolonged and serious this time around. Students refused to go to classes for at least a portion of three days, and some marched the five miles or so from our school to the county school administration building in Trenton. On the final day of the walkouts, the protesters blocked the main hallway at school and did some violence to the building. The principal called for help from the local sheriff's office, though our sheriff, famous for being drunk all day and for not much more than that, was not likely much help under the circumstances. The superintendent ordered schools closed in the county, and they remained so for a week.

At the same time, a freak snowstorm hit eastern North Carolina, dumping inches of snow onto the villages, roads, and fields.

In my memory, the snow became the reason that school was closed; such a large snowfall would certainly have prevented schools from operating for part of the period. I thought of the walkout as simply more evidence of the trouble between black students and the faculty. By the time we returned to school, in my memory, Mr. Fleming had won an appeal to retain his job, and the issue was resolved.

The facts were different, however, as I learned when I studied articles printed in the *Kinston Daily Free Press*. The Kinston paper circulated in the portion of the county around Trenton; in Pollocksville, we were more likely to read the *Sun Journal*, the New Bern paper, which offered little or no coverage of the problems in Jones County schools. (In my household, we read no newspaper at all, so I would not have known what was in them in any case.)

From the newspapers, I learned a number of details that I did not know at the time. It was from the news reports that I learned that schools were closed because of the unrest in our high school and not because of the snow. The paper recorded details about the firing of Mr. Fleming, the claim that he had failed some evaluations and refused to participate in others, as well as the claim made by his students that he was fired because he had mixed sex education with work on arithmetic during class.

I also learned about an open forum that took place during the days when school was closed. As part of the investigation into the walkout and the violence at school, the superintendent and principal held a public meeting in Trenton, and many parents attended. I have no memory of this meeting at all, and do not believe I ever heard about it at the time. My mother remembers nothing about this meeting either. So I have no idea how it was scheduled or how parents learned about it.

The newspaper reported this event in some detail. The discussion was lively and exposed a number of issues. Parents and students claimed that the school administration was not listening to their wishes. School administration claimed that neither parents nor students had expressed any wishes. Most people at the meeting agreed that the Parent-Teacher Associations had died out in the aftermath of integration. Mr. Cooper, the high school principal, noted with some frustration that parents were not supporting the high school at all. He implied that the problems of integration were being solved by the administrators, teachers, and students, without much input from the community.

Students countered that Mr. Cooper himself was part of the problem, since he offered little or no communication with students himself. They pointed out that student government was mostly inactive.

Everyone agreed that the problems at the high school were largely between black students, faculty, and administration; the white and black students were getting along pretty well, and had accepted integration without much fuss.

When school resumed, the county hired a number of adults to patrol the halls and open areas. The teachers requested this protection, fearing anger from the student body. I do recall the guards, and the uncertainty of our teachers. But classes resumed without incident.

This year, however, the principal and administration took more action than they had in the first year. We elected representatives to student government, one from each homeroom class, and the student body president, Andy Norton, led meetings during which we discussed what had happened. I was part of the group and was assigned to write a new constitution for student government, to help make its workings regular, and to give it some independence from school administration. No such document existed before.

According to the newspapers, seventy black students were suspended for their participation in the walkouts, and one student was prosecuted for trespassing when he refused to leave school grounds after being suspended. Our student government discussed the justice of these suspensions, though I have no recollection of the number of students being mentioned, and was surprised to learn later that the number was so high. Student government voted that the student suspensions should not be enforced. Black students voted against the suspensions, and white students voted for them. There were two exceptions—Eben Strahan, a black football player, voted with the white students, and I voted with the black students.

The discussions in student government eased any tensions that might have existed between black and white students, if there were any in the first place. White students as a whole had no sympathy with the walkouts, which they called riots; but they had no real stake in them, either.

The Kinston paper noted that three white students were injured at the peak of the protests. If this was the case, I never heard any details. If true, this would likely have led to further tension between students, especially if the injuries were severe or deliberate. But for the rest of the school year, we students got along as well as we had before, and white people mostly snickered about the protests, repeating the story from the previous year, that black students had just wanted to get out of school for a few days.

Mr. Fleming agreed to undergo teaching evaluations and to cooperate with the administration, so he returned to his duties.

NEITHER I NOR any of my white friends became involved in the walkouts. None of my black friends ever talked to me about the issues that made them angry. These facts are illustrative of the degree to which cross-racial friendships remained tentative and incomplete, no matter how genuine the affection between the parties. No matter how good-hearted I might be, no matter how willing I thought I was to engage with my friends, I was still white, and whiteness was still a problem for all my black friends. So it would remain.

Would I have demonstrated with my friends, had they asked? In my particular case, the answer is very likely no. My hemophilia would have stopped me. Had I not been a free bleeder, would I have joined them? The answer would probably have been the same, though I would very much like to pretend otherwise.

Did my black friends want white allies in their fight? I would guess that they did not, since they never asked, and since, when the walkouts happened, black students often warned their white friends to steer clear of the action. Even more important, these students had no reason to trust white people to take part in a healthy way, and every reason to believe that involving us might lead to negative consequences. I suspect their parents counseled against inviting white students, maybe for fear of awakening greater animosity among white adults.

In both these years, when students demonstrated, they did so for concrete reasons. The causes of the walkouts were documented in at least the one local newspaper. Yet among white people, the facts never took hold, and we spoke of the events as riots, attributing the cause to whatever came to mind that fit our prejudice. Black students just wanted to get out of school for a few days at exam time. I heard this more than once, at the time and in later years, when in fact the walkouts took place in late February, long after exams were over.

God Gave Me a Song

O ur high school had a chorus of black students who sang gospel music, and the chorus featured Violet Strahan, my classmate from sixth grade, who had a powerful singing voice. The chorus occupied its own mobile classroom at the end of a long plank boardwalk, and its members practiced in the chorus for one full class period every day. I remember this chorus from my junior year in high school, though likely it was in place during my sophomore year, too. By senior year there was no more choir by virtue of the fact that the student in charge of the class had graduated—a very gifted student, Isaac Urban, who had taught himself to play the piano at a very young age, and who would go on to a career as a composer, singer, and musician.

The chorus was likely a relic of the old black high school, and its place in the new high school came about as a result of that. I suspect it was Isaac's passion for music that preserved the chorus. There had been no school chorus at the white high school, and perhaps this explains why there were no white students in the chorus.

The choir was a matter of pride for our school, as was Isaac, his maturity, and his genius at music. They competed in local gospel chorus competitions and did very well.

When I heard the chorus rehearse, I sometimes envied them. But I never had the impulse to try to join the class. White teenagers were not allowed to aspire to become members of black gospel choirs. Neither group would have liked it much. White people already feared that the government would force integration onto churches next, and if that happened, then surely the end of time would follow. Black people already felt the loss of their own schools and the community that had come together to support them.

There were still strong prohibitions in place as to how much association whites and blacks were allowed outside of school. Most extracurricular activities were integrated to some degree, though few of these clubs or groups involved much in the way of social activity. The athletic teams drew almost entirely from the black student population, with one or two white students participating in most sports. The high school basketball team, our mighty Trojans, had two white members in my junior year, both of whom rode with the principal when they went to away games, avoiding the ride with their black teammates on the school's activity bus.

In these years, the school revived the Beta Club, a society

for students with good grades, though the membership comprised mostly white students. The Beta Club involved a certain amount of social activity, including a trip to the state Beta Club convention that involved our staying overnight in Raleigh, some two hours away by car. We managed this trip without any resistance on the part of parents or people in the community. The fact that this was a trip for smart students in some way defined it as acceptable, not too radical, even though black students and white students were sleeping in the same building, side by side.

Other groups and clubs took on a different balance. Wherever one race predominated, there was a strong possibility that the minority would endure a good deal of bullying.

The gospel chorus sang for the school at assemblies in the gymnasium. At an assembly in the spring, near the end of the term, they performed "God Gave Me a Song," written by renowned gospel singer Myrna Summers. The song featured a simple, passionate lyric; the choir was powerful and clear, with Violet singing the lead in a voice that simply swelled around us, ringing from the girders of the gym roof. Isaac moved from side to side on his piano bench, lifting one hand from time to time to make a small gesture that directed the singers. Placed at the center of the choir, Violet's round face, small chin, and intense eyes gave over to the song, the sound pouring out of her like a force. "God gave me a song that the angels cannot sing." I had never quite lost my fear of her, and she continued to make it clear that she wanted little or nothing to do with white people. When I remember her, I remember first her anger when I called her a name in sixth grade, and then I remember her voice singing this song in high school.

Watching the chorus, I also wanted to sing that song, raise my voice. I pictured myself as one of the singers. This was not out of any solidarity, any budding social consciousness or desire to push the boundary of social equality. My wish sprang more from vanity, from wishing to be part of this sound, wishing that it might fill me, that I might participate in it.

Were I writing a book of fiction I might pretend that I had sung with that chorus, since the memory of the moment is so vivid even after the passage of so much time. At least I might report that I had made a brave effort to become a member of the chorus, earning the trust of the other black students, and in the process becoming a beacon of change, a little white hero. But in fact I had accepted the status quo, for the most part. I was willing to edge myself toward the limits of what was acceptable, but no further.

In a novel or film, the character who was me would have taken that moment and found purpose from it. Brave and preternaturally confident, he would have asked to be in the choir, made a place for himself in those voices, sung beside Violet, moving as she did, proving that the separation between the races could one day be conquered. He would have overcome all obstacles, including the skepticism of the teachers, the principal, the resistance of his parents, the mockery of the students on both sides of the color line, all to prove that true unity and community were possible. In the movie, he would have been the best chorus member of all. I can spin this fantasy quite easily as I write, knowing as I do that such a thought never occurred to me at the time. I had adapted myself to hiding, and my only real ambition for high school, and for Jones County, was to survive and escape. I had too many secrets to be brave.

Even while I was taking some risks in school by siding with black students on issues like those related to the protests, I was only changing my own attitudes to the degree that I needed to do so. Race was still, for all its importance, only part of the life I had to lead. I had made some choices, seen the reality of discrimination, and come to some marginal understanding of its impact on the world. I had come to understand my part in the problem of skin color, had learned some ways to subvert my tendencies toward prejudice. But I made these changes in myself only because integration happened, only because I had consequently grown to know black people as friends and equals, at least within the sphere of equality that school provided. I had learned to listen and had made a kind of commitment to believe, always, that black people were telling the truth about racism, and white people were not.

This was surrounded, however, by all the rest of my life, the realities I lived with, including the fact that I was gay and in hiding, the continuing collapse of my parents' marriage, my father's mental illness, my brother's much more serious hemophilia, conflicts between my sister and mother, my urgent need to write, all the books I read, and the fact that I would leave home in a year, headed to college. I was self-absorbed, sometimes dangerously so. The world and all its troubles often felt unreal. Only the world inside my head mattered, and I hid in there as much as I could.

Still, I would like to have lived in a world where I could have sung in that chorus, where what mattered would have been only the way my voice blended with the others and the sound we made. I think I could have added to the music.

The Smoking Patio

At some point in the spring of that year, it had become clear to all that Mercy and Andy had fallen in love with each other. I had known Andy for a year or so, Mercy for two. Her family was old and prominent, though still poor, and included an eccentric judge who was our county's only novelist. She had grown up on integrated military bases all over the world, only to move to Trenton, where she learned that God had intended the races to live separate from one another. Andy was the student body president, a member of the football team, one of the most popular people around. He had grown up in Trenton. That he was attracted to Mercy became clear after a short bit of flirting. That Mercy returned the attraction was plain to those of us who knew her. She had a sharp tongue, long legs, a mellow presence. In the art of verbal sparring she gave as good as she got. Andy had a breathy voice, a handsome face, a gentle laugh, and a clown's willingness to please.

One of the places where they came in contact was outside the cafeteria after lunch, when smokers gathered to inhale their cigarettes. On the smoking patio, Andy could flit from his main group of friends to our group by taking only a few steps.

Their courtship played itself out in front of all the smokers, and for that reason they contained their attraction and made it as tidy and unobtrusive as they could. They liked each other, talked, kept closer to one another than anyone else, but went no further in public. This was enough, under the watchful eyes of the other students, to start rumors and to create a bit of scandal.

Mercy's father owned the small restaurant in Trenton and was a committed segregationist, a drunkard, and a bully. Part of what had drawn the two of us into friendship was the fact that our fathers were similar, and we could share this with one another. In all my life I'd had no one to whom I could talk about the problems my father caused. Queen of sarcasm though Mercy might be in some settings, she was a good friend, and once we knew we lived under the thumb of similar bullies, we relied on each other.

She would face real trouble if this courtship with Andy became known to her family. We knew this at the time and dealt with it to the degree that we understood it. On the smoking patio, our group of hippy imitators provided a bit of cover, since at least a small group of people were usually involved in integrated conversation. We provided a context in which the two of them could talk to one another without drawing more attention than was wise.

"This is just fucked up," Mercy said. She could swear and make the words sound natural; people always giggled when I tried to cuss. "This place is so fucked up. I like this guy and I'm not supposed to do anything about it."

"That is messed up," Barbara agreed. We were standing near one of the picnic tables on the patio.

"I can't wait to get out of this place."

"One more year."

I generally kept quiet when the topic of conversation turned to romance. That was probably the year I dated Becky Howard exactly once. She was the second girl I had dated, a pleasant, agreeable person, and I enjoyed the afternoon. But I had not liked holding her hand, and knew I never would. I had decided I never wanted to date a girl again. I saw no reason to pretend otherwise.

STUDENTS WERE ALLOWED to smoke cigarettes on a patio outside the lunchroom, a concrete slab surrounded by a low brick wall. Because some of my friends were smokers, I often accompanied them to inhale their secondhand smoke, a term unheard of at the time. I had escaped any desire to inhale nicotine, but a large percentage of my schoolmates were smokers, or had friends who smoked, making the patio a lively place. This was the era in which the link between tobacco and cancer was being made explicit, but hardly anyone cared. Many of the students came from families who raised tobacco, or who worked in tobacco in some fashion, its being a reliable and profitable crop. Cancer was our business and our livelihood; tobacco money flowed through the pockets of all our parents in one way or another.

By its nature, enjoying cigarettes was an integrated activity at our school, since there was only one smoking area and all the tobacco addicts had to share it. The patio was a cool place to spend the minutes after we scraped our plates and separated our silverware from plasticware at the dishwashing station. We sat on picnic tables or stood near them, fists shoved into jeans, our hair longer than our parents', even in rural North Carolina where no one wanted to be thought a hippy. We gazed across the flat field adjacent to the school, across the broken cornstalks to a distant line of hedge and a barrier of sentinel pines.

While we students shared the space, black and white groups demarked their own neighborhoods within it, white sitting with white, black sitting with black, some of us mingling, the core of each group posing with their cigarettes, inhaling, blowing smoke, tapping ash. The cigarette was an easy kind of prop for the movie of living, and gave the hands and the mouth something to do that created a sense of self-satisfaction and ease. The smokers appeared to be mugging for an invisible camera.

Rhonda and Ursula accompanied their boyfriends to the smoking patio sometimes. They never smoked themselves, and so while their boyfriends were occupied, they circulated and talked. This was one of the ways we maintained the friendships we had begun years earlier. We talked about music, especially soul music, and Vietnam, and the way that Mr. Riggs, our math teacher, pulled up his pants so high that his belt wrapped just beneath his lungs. We talked about who was in love, who was breaking up, who had been caught cheating on his or her steady mate. Classes, colleges, clothes, music, makeup, what we might do on a weekend. I joined the conversations that were safe for me, avoided the ones that touched on my secrets. Since I had no steady girlfriend, I had to plot a cautious path, aware that most of the boys, white and black, considered me to be a sissy, and possibly something much worse—in their eyes, if not in mine.

MERCY AND ANDY were not the only couple who were flirting across the color line. I remember three couples from the time who were meeting in secret, all involving young black men and white women; and I recall one pair, a white boy and a black girl, who had a long flirtation that went nowhere. As I have already noted, at least one of my black friends was impersonating me in order to call a white girl with whom he wanted to flirt; she had been my girlfriend briefly in elementary school, in the days when we passed notes with boxes that said CHECK YES OR NO. There was also a hidden romance among two teachers, Mrs.

Osterman and Mr. Byrd; she would leave her husband for him the next year, thus costing the county two good teachers, since they moved to another part of the state.

All these people were my friends and in some cases I helped them to meet outside school. Once I went to a drive-in movie with Priscilla Potter and Georganne Clark, whose boyfriend, Earl, joined us in the car at the movie, the two of them taking the back seat, doing their business as the movie unfolded. I stared at the screen intently, pretending not to hear what was happening behind me in the dark. The drive-in theaters in Kinston and New Bern were convenient for this kind of rendezvous, since cars offered some privacy and concealment. The worst exposure was the moment of getting into or out of the car, when other people could see who was who.

Earl and Georganne also hung out on the smoking patio, though they, like Mercy and Andy, kept their feelings for each other low key. They could not spend their time together openly, or declare themselves to be officially going steady or even dating. We were still living in a South that avenged such relationships, and in the past, the punishments had been murderous. I heard rumors of cross burnings from black students now and then. I knew that black men were accused of rape when caught consorting with a white woman, and that white men punished this by lynching.

The patio provided the kind of setting that white segregationists had always feared, an arena in which whites and blacks could mingle as equals. While the groups did segregate, and each attempted to assert some kind of superiority, there was none to be had. The space belonged to both groups equally. Both needed it enough not to endanger access by any serious misbehavior. The addiction to nicotine trumped the need to maintain de facto borders and a wider separation. The students coexisted without much incident, even around the weeks of the riot. There was likely some mouthing off from time to time. I witnessed nothing memorable.

Even people who supported integration might balk at inter-racial couples. Once again we had strayed into the territory of, "But would you want your sister to marry one?" I heard that phrase often enough during those years, framed sometimes as a statement and sometimes as a question, though the idea remained the same. There was equality and then there was the territory beyond. The question probed for a common ground of separation. Surely no white person wanted to be kin to a Negro? Surely no Caucasian brother, no matter how liberal he might be, wanted his sister to be married to a black man?

The phrase, mentioning always the sister and never any other relation, presented itself as essentially masculine. Was the brother then to be free to marry whomever he pleased? Was he to decide the disposition of his sister in the end? Approve her choice of mates?

In reaching for a new order of the world, in ending Jim Crow and beginning to face the idea of true equality among all people, were white liberals abandoning all ideas of color and difference? Was everybody to be allowed to date everybody? Was the sister to be allowed freedom to choose her own mate? Was this not chaos?

On the smoking patio, attempting to appear older and cooler, comfortable with ourselves, we acted out old rituals of flirtation amid a new social order. We did so in a compressed space where the smokers competed for a stage, a place from which to pose. In spite of the refusal of the races to mix completely, we were likely no more sullen or vain than any set of teenagers had ever been. By now the fact of mixed schools had become ordinary, to a degree. We were learning to live with this new pattern. We had courtships and mating to carry on, and these needs overshadowed everything else.

As I observed in the hours of watching my friends smoke, I noted the ebb and flow of all the groups, fluid clusters of people drawn together by an idea of comfort. It would be naïve to describe this interaction as of two groups, or three; the black people were hardly homogenous, nor were the white people. The set of students who mixed across the color line was neither fixed nor isolated in any way, and people of both races, sometimes shyly, moved into and out of this space.

I watched all this with such detachment as I could muster. There were no longer any boys in school to whom I was drawn; I allowed no such feelings to evolve. I hung out on the smoking patio but smoked no cigarettes; I hung out with couples but showed no interest in love. Other people likely knew this was a pretense, but no one bothered me.

I watched Mercy and Andy, envying the gentleness of their interactions, the cautiousness of their approach to one another. As to the details of their feelings, I knew only what I saw. Mercy was never one to talk about herself very much, and what I learned came out in bits and pieces. They talked by phone. They met where they could. They kept the secret of their closeness through the rest of that year. Then, at last, summer came, and we had only one more year of high school to go.

Horizons

During my last year in high school, and what would prove to be my last year in Jones County, I recall turmoil that had more to do with my life than with questions of race. My father's drinking had driven him into rehabilitation, and then into a new job. My parents' marriage was beginning to unravel in a way that looked to be permanent. I had spent the summer away from home, at Governor's School, and Mercy, with whom I had become close, was unhappy at home and thinking about moving out.

It is hard to recall at my present age how long and slow were the weeks and months when I was seventeen. Even the thought of waiting a single year to graduate from high school felt dense and thankless, especially when so many chapters of my early life were closing. My parents were divorcing. My sister had left for college, heading to East Carolina University to study nursing. Our family became smaller and quieter.

The summer between junior and senior years of high school was dominated by the weeks I spent at Governor's School, a program for smart students run in Winston-Salem, across the state a good ways to the west. At Governor's School I was granted a taste of freedom, a few weeks' exposure to a city, a few weeks in which I did not have to worry about my father's drinking, a time when I could be around people my age who were also smart. I glimpsed the world beyond Jones County and understood myself to be a part of it. I began to say good-bye to my old home.

The school lasted for six weeks during the middle of the summer, housed on the campus of Salem College in the old Moravian neighborhood of Salem. I was roommates with one of the members of the chorus, music being one of the several areas of study in which a student could be chosen to attend the school. Our room, small and plastered, with one window, was on the third floor of Clewell dormitory, and on the first day, when my mother had dropped me off and headed home on the drive of four hours or so, I lay on my narrow bed and listened to the other students settling into their rooms. I had a curious sense of lightness and homesickness, a quickness, as if I could rise from the bed and drift anywhere I chose, and a dread that I had lost all the life I had lived before that moment. My past had dissolved into the east somewhere. A place where I had spent nearly seventeen years had dwindled to tiny size, to be replaced by this one, where I had my own bed and took my meals in a cafeteria and had nothing to worry about except the classes I was expected to attend.

Freedom for me consisted of nothing but the ability to remove myself from conflicts brought into my life by other people. It was as simple as having a bed of my own in a dormitory and enough separation from my old life that it could not reach me. My mother wrote me every day. I was happy for the letters and missed her from time to time, but otherwise thought of nothing concerning home. I had entered this world-within-a-world and I had embraced it.

The place was ideal in some ways, meant to reaffirm the value of having a strong mind when the culture at large often appeared more concerned with looks or athletic prowess, wealth or good family. We attended classes in our specialty, English being mine, but also went through a process akin to group therapy, doing exercises aimed at probing our differences, our prejudices, our pains. Our last sessions involved the study of F. S. C. Northrop, a philosopher, and his theories of knowledge. I had strengths for English and group therapy but no real grasp of Northrop.

The group of students was of mixed skin color to a small degree, but it had been years since I sat in class with so many white students. Here in Governor's School I met my friend Sheria, with whom I would later attend college. She was African-American, smart as a whip, more fun to talk to than almost anybody I had ever met, making one joke after another, though sometimes with a kind of desperate edge. I think we under-stood each other's fear. We were both the products of deeply unhappy homes, as we would learn later.

I met other boys who were like me, and we talked around the issue, though never openly. In Clewell dorm I was teased about being a sissy and one boy harassed me every time he got the chance, asked me whether I would like to put his dick in my mouth, crude and leering, a pudgy fellow with black glasses and weak, owlish eyes. Finally at the end of the session I exploded and screamed at him that it was none of his business what I was and that if I wanted to suck somebody's dick it would not be his. After that he sobered and later apologized for having spent so much energy in tormenting me. I understood he had meant no harm, and I think I knew that all along. He was picking at me in order to make himself fit into the group of boys, all of whom had spotted me for one of the sissies, a probable queer. He was not alone in calling me names, but he was the loudest and most persistent.

At Governor's School I came to understand that groups choose to ridicule and exclude certain people in order to de-fine themselves, in order to create a sense of commonality. By teasing the sissies, including me, the other boys bonded and formed a group. Not all of them, of course, but enough. In fact, this process is often institutionalized, fraternities being a good example. No group is worth joining if everybody is welcome. The notion of a world of equals is not nearly as interesting as a world ruled from the top down. Every group comes with a built-in presumption of its own superiority.

Having been invited to a gathering of students who were intelligent, I began to understand the need to go even further in terms of thinking for myself and making my own choices. So it was that I learned to make friends there and move freely among the students in spite of the fact that some of them liked to call me names. I learned to toughen my skin a bit. This was probably what my high school would have felt like but for the shock brought on by integration. Had there been a greater diversity of students at Governor's School, had its racial mix more resembled that of the state from which the student body was drawn, I wonder whether the gang of boys would have felt so free to make my life unpleasant. I suspect that different racial groups of boys would have been, instead, preoccupied with posturing for one another.

By the time I returned to Jones County, I was changed in some fundamental way. With my suitcases I walked into the front door of my house, looked at my mother and burst into tears. "Mama, I was so happy there," I said, maybe the cruelest moment I ever put her through. She understood that I could not be happy to come home, no matter how much I had missed my family. It was not so much the place that I had enjoyed as the freedom; I had found the independence addictive, so that for the remainder of my senior year I had one foot already across the county line. I was already fleeing.

I wanted to leave not because of Jones County or its people, not because of the constrictions of the life there, not because of the quiet. It was my family and its troubles I wanted to escape more than anything else. This being the case, I was also torn by guilt at the thought of leaving my mother and brothers, at the fact that my mother was losing all her children, that soon she would have nothing but my father and that house and that town. Yet most of my life I had been told I would grow up and leave Jones County, that there was little to keep me there, that I would go to college and become something or other and never look back.

As for my family, that issue quickly took a turn that I had thought would never happen, the final separation of my parents. My father had spent part of the year in an alcohol rehabilitation center. He stopped drinking for a while, and then, suddenly, his will simply collapsed. He gave up working at all. He moved from his chair in the living room to the bedroom, where he slept a good deal. With the rest of us he took on a childlike affect, asking us in a high-pitched whine to bring him Pepsi-Colas from the corner filling station, for instance, doing so every time one of us left the house. However, a few weeks after that, the drinking started again.

After so many years of his drinking and bullying, my mother had reached the end of her ability to cope. In past days she had endured his bad treatment because she felt she had no other choice, and, in truth, divorce was never an option for a person who wanted a good reputation in Pollocksville. My father had always managed to keep a job and bring money into the house. But now he was no longer working, and my mother understood that she would have to take care of our family on her own. So she found a way to put him out of the house for good. When he drank and started quarrels with her, she fought back in ways he had never expected, throwing pots of coffee at him, breaking dishes, screaming at him till she was red-faced and shaking. On the last day my father lived with us, she collapsed, as if she were truly losing her mind, after a fit of fury at my father, who was, by then, drinking as heavily as ever and adding pills to the mix when he could. I took my mother to the local doctor, a man who finally listened to her and took a step that ended my parents' marriage of nearly twenty years. The doctor called Aunt Dora and told her she had to get my father out of our house. Whatever he said to my aunt, she listened. She had known this day was coming, I don't doubt. My father's family had helped us when they could, and knew the kind of trouble into which he was descending. A couple of hours later Aunt Dora showed up with my uncle and took my father home with her.

With this exit began a drama in which my father would attempt to return to our house over and over, only to be rebuffed. In the midst of this chaos, I entered twelfth grade. This was the fall of 1972, another election year, with the war in Vietnam providing a bloody backdrop, and the draft threatening every eighteen-year-old with military service, as it had for all the years

I could remember. The war had overshadowed the civil rights movement by then, though the two were never entirely separate, since part of the reason for continued African-American violence was the fact that African-American sons and daughters had served and died in Vietnam in numbers much larger than their proportion in the population. This was especially true during the Johnson years. The war had eaten at our faith in nearly everything, from government to the military itself. I had written a term paper during my junior year about the massacre of civilians at My Lai. My friends had peace symbols on their army fatigue jackets and their ripped jeans. We wanted McGovern to win the presidential election but we knew he would not.

We were old enough to think we mattered, and to have opinions, though it was not cool to dwell on such things. What was cool was to keep up with rock bands, to flaunt our friendships across the color lines, to smoke marijuana in secret, and to wear bell-bottomed jeans that looked as though they had never been washed. I don't speak of myself as a wearer of cool clothing, however. I was still carrying a good deal of baby fat, I had a red bush of hair, and my clothes were mostly bought in company with my mother during a two-day flurry of back-to-school shopping, thus limiting any idea I might have had of self-expression through dress. Truth is that I had no such sense of clothing and have labored all my life with a crippling indolence of taste. I can remember one pair of pants in which I often went to school during my senior year, a rust-brown plaid that must have been a complete eyesore, the cuffs a bit short since I was still growing, my body shaped like a spindle with thread wrapped thickest around the middle. I hated having to tuck my shirt into my britches because I felt my belly hanging over my belt all day. My connection to my body was tenuous, and my opinion of it quite low.

While I continued in friendships with the same core group of students who were actually attempting to integrate, the group itself was changed by the exit of the previous year's graduates and the addition of cherubs from the sophomore class. All my friends were older and had changed, same as I had changed, and maybe I looked the same to them as they appeared to me. I saw my peers as harder, colder, more distant and skeptical, not of me but of the school, of the place we lived. Our school had a new principal and some new teachers, including a new crop of servicemen's wives from Camp LeJeune and Cherry Point. There were enough out-siders on the faculty now that the old-time teachers who hailed from the county might easily have felt threatened. Tensions re-mained between the Afro-American students and the faculty, a feeling that last year's violence had done no good.

Conversations were starting that would continue for de-cades. Student tracking, the separation of students into those who had college potential and those who did not, was used as a way to segregate classrooms once again. It had ensured that I never sat in a classroom in which I was in the minority. Black teachers were losing their jobs and school boards were claiming that there were not enough qualified black teachers to provide the needed balance of numbers, so most school faculties had a majority of white teachers. Segregation had suffered a defeat but had not ended.

As for my friendships from that elementary school class at Alex H. White, the group with whom I had begun school twelve years before, these had become little more than memory. We had lost each other. The old tradition of white solidarity had cracked, although it still had a good deal of vitality. But we were the faces of the students who had done the work of integrating the schools.

For everyone, there was a certain degree of bitterness involved in the realization that the consolidation of the black and white school systems had likely caused as many problems as it had solved. This need not have been the case. Had the adults all chosen to accept and support the new schools, our county would have been a different place. It is certain that segregation had to end, and equally certain that the end could have come about in a better way.

Still, even when seen with all its flaws, the fact of integration, the end of the separate-but-equal school systems, was enormous. I have no idea what kind of person I would have been had I not lived through those years.

As IF TO express her irony, nature provided me with a certain kind of cover during my senior year, and I kept my secret to the end.

Priscilla Potter, originally my sister's friend in elementary school and now my friend, too, started inviting me to go out on the weekends, not on dates but rather on adventures that made me feel almost like a normal teenager. We traveled to Kinston to watch Lamar Vickers's band. Once she drove me to pick up Ursula Doleman and Peter Strahan, and we went to New Bern and drove around awhile, then came home. By the following Monday the rumor had flown through school that Priscilla had been dating Peter, and I had been dating Ursula, two interracial couples in one car, the sort of sin that by rights ought to have caused an explosion in the vehicle, at the very least.

This story came out in advanced math class, when Mr. Riggs had stepped out of the room. I first heard a kind of buzz of conversation, as I was daydreaming about a boy I had met at Governor's School. Something pulled me out of the fantasy: Delores Rickets, who sat in front of me, looked at me somberly. "I am so disappointed in you," she said.

I realized that everybody was staring at me except Ursula, who had her head bowed and was staring at her desk.

"What?" I asked.

Several voices spoke at once about seeing us in New Bern and me and Ursula in the backseat of the car, and I realized what had happened.

My remaining white friends from elementary school were mostly in that class, and they shook their heads. The black kids were upset with Ursula, as her boyfriend would later be. No one bothered to ask what had actually happened. It was apparently too much to conceive that we were simply friends who pre-ferred, that night, each other's company, largely out of boredom with staying at home.

It felt somehow right that the black girl I was supposed to have dated was Ursula, who had kissed me on the cheek in seventh grade. There was comedy in the fact that the people who called me sissy behind my back also condemned me for interracial (and heterosexual) dating.

Mercy

One weekend during the fall of senior year, Mercy and I were invited to East Carolina University for a recruitment event aimed at gifted students in the region. Neither of us had any plans to attend ECU for college, but we accepted the invitation because it meant two nights away from home. For Mercy, this was also a chance to spend time with Andy, and I could provide her with a certain level of camouflage if I went with her. I am tempted to say it was she who convinced me to go on the trip, since that is the way I would write the story if I were making it up. But I can't have been that hard to convince. Governor's School had given me a taste of the independence I craved, and this weekend on a college campus might reinforce the lesson.

We took a bus to Greenville, a little over an hour's drive from Trenton, and attended orientation for the weekend's recruiting events. Once we had our keys and room assignments, we headed to our rooms. Mercy had a room in Cotten Hall, one of the older buildings on the quad. I dumped my little suitcase in the room I was supposed to share for the weekend with one of the upperclassmen. He was asleep on his bed. I set my belongings on the other bed, guessing it to be mine. Then I headed back to Cotten Hall.

In Mercy's room, large and high-ceilinged, she told me that her roommate was gone for the weekend, and she had the whole room to herself. "Can you believe it?" She had a glittery, almost feverish look in her eyes at the prospect. "Is that luck or what?"

"My roommate was asleep. I didn't even talk to him."

"Andy is about to get here. Oh, my goodness." She sat on her bed and bounced a bit.

"Does he know how to find you?"

"We're going to meet him in front of the dorm," she said.

"Great."

"You want to get stoned tonight? You want to try pot?"

This was that moment I had waited for all my life, peer pressure to do drugs. I caved in right away, shrugging, trying to look as cool as possible. "Sure."

She laughed, a sound with a bit of a maniacal edge. Here we were, prisoners of Jones County, escaped for a few hours, and about to do as we pleased.

Andy and the people he had come to visit met us after dark, and we took a ride with them to a field outside of Greenville.

In those days a car could easily fit three passengers in both front and back seats, and the car was full. Andy introduced us all and we sat in the dark, quietly passing a joint, Andy and the others sharing a bottle of Boone's Farm wine. The wine was wrapped in a brown paper sack that rustled as it passed from hand to hand.

"Jimmy is getting stoned," Andy said, and giggled, passing the joint to me.

I grinned in the dark, inhaled, the strong taste of the smoke filling my head.

"It doesn't always work the first time you smoke it," Mercy warned.

One of the guys in the backseat agreed.

But it worked fine.

We drove back to campus and said good-bye to Andy's friends. I hung out in the room with Andy and Mercy for a while; Mercy kept her eye on me, feeling a bit protective or responsible, maybe. I had started to giggle and could not stop. I kept repeating, "This is amazing," and giggling some more, wiggling my fingers from time to time.

Mercy and Andy were spooning on the other bed. They were quietly resting against each other, their voices all murmur and softness.

It seemed an eternity passed. I realized I needed to leave and stood, more or less steady on my feet, gathering my courage, reasonably certain I could find the dorm where I was staying.

"You leaving?" Mercy asked, raising up her head from Andy's shoulder.

"I think so."

"You're fucked up, Jimmy," Andy said. "You're going to get lost."

"No, I'm not." I heaved myself toward the door, the motion feeling so odd. My head was gliding but my feet were plodding.

"Be careful. Come back here if you can't find your room."

"I'll be fine," I said.

Mercy settled against Andy again as I closed the door behind me. I stumbled into the dark, took a couple of wrong turns, giggled a good deal, and eventually found the dorm where I was staying for the night. My roommate was still asleep in the room, more or less in the same position as before.

Mercy and I never spoke about whether they were having sex, though I would guess from things that Mercy told me later that they were not. I have no idea whether they ever crossed into that territory. Mercy was not one to share her life unnecessarily.

This weekend sealed my friendship with Mercy, and after it, we talked regularly at school about Andy, about her home life and mine. A couple of times I visited her in Trenton, meeting her mother and her little sister, her brother and even her father, who had the gaunt, pop-eyed look of a drinking man. Lean and tough as whipcord, like my own father. When Mercy could no longer tolerate living under the same roof with him, I helped her move into her grandmother's place, a house a couple of blocks away in Trenton.

Only a few weeks before school ended, Mercy's grandmother died, and her family moved into the house where she had lived. Mercy and her father quarreled, and Mercy moved out, living with her sister in Kinston for the rest of the year. She rode to high school with one of our teachers.

Almost our last act as friends in high school was to escort one another to the prom. I had made no plans to go, since I had given up dating after those two dates. Mercy and I were part of the group who decorated the gym, though, and we decided we might as well go to the prom since we'd done so much work to get ready for it. We made the decision only a few days before, and I wore a suit rather than a tuxedo, picking Mercy up at her house, taking her to the dance, then, later, taking her to rendez-vous with Andy, with whom she had arranged to spend the end of prom night. We had been a cute fake couple, we thought. My last memory of the evening was the happiness on her face as she stepped into the car with Andy.

Sometime after school ended, the two of them lost touch with each other. Mercy made it to Chapel Hill a year later than me, and Andy was there, too. But he wanted little to do with white people by then; I learned this from Mercy many years later. At the time, she just shrugged and moved forward.

Commencement

At graduation, student body president Stella Newman spoke to the crowd in the gymnasium. She said the sorts of things that one usually says in graduation speeches, and whatever I once remembered of the content has been erased. I wonder what of our real experience there she chose to mark. What I remember is sitting among my classmates, knowing the ordeal had come to an end. I shook hands with people, milled among them, felt a stirring of sadness at moments, but never for very long. My family waited patiently till I was ready and we drove home from the school. I was leaving it for the last time. Most of those people, with whom I had lived an intense drama, a piece of history, I never saw again.

In the fall I attended university in Chapel Hill, coming home to Pollocksville twice more, once for Thanksgiving and once for Christmas. At the end of Christmas, my mother met a man with whom she fell in love, and she moved our family to Goldsboro to be with him. She had already divorced my father. She took this step knowing that the people of Pollocksville would gossip, that any respectability we had established would vanish, and that any tenuous welcome we had enjoyed there would come to an end. She didn't care anymore. She saw her future elsewhere. So we left Jones County for good.

There was never a moment when I decided that I would not go back to eastern North Carolina to live. I remained for a long time a creature who looked only barely past the horizon. In Chapel Hill I studied and built a self, learned to love my freedom, and made some steps toward understanding how to live as a gay man. After Chapel Hill I moved to New Orleans in order to live among gay people for a while. Years went by, I only went back to North Carolina from time to time, and home was no longer Jones County.

Reunion

———————

Decades later, I am driving toward Jones County once again, headed for the forty-year reunion of the class of 1973. Late August heat weighs over the highway, but I am proof against summer in the cocoon of the car, and the flat fields of eastern North Carolina are thick with corn, cotton in bloom or in bales, tobacco yet to be harvested. The land wants rain, the sky is enormous, filling most of the world, just as I remember from years ago when this countryside was all I knew.

I learned about the class reunion via social media, where I have reconnected after a fashion with people from my past: college, family, high school, elementary school, and various jobs. I peer at pictures of my friends, straining to see the younger face in the older. They all look so old on Facebook, I wonder how they can bear it. Whereas I am certain I look more or less the same.

It has been a season of reunions of one kind or another as I draw near to sixty, gathering the loose threads of a lifetime, trying to understand what meaning can be woven of them. I have been remembering so deeply, even dreaming of places I left behind when my life in Jones County ended: the cramped green house on Barrus Street in Pollocksville, the railroad trestle that has been torn down, the overgrown riverbank where I sat and dropped stones into the dark water.

While I've returned regularly to this part of North Carolina, I've only made the trip to my old home place a handful of times; when my family moved from the town during my freshman year of college, I lost my link to Jones County. Chapel Hill took me over so completely that I felt as if I had been born there. I turned my back on rural life, figuring there was no place for me in it. My family settled in North Carolina in the counties where my mother grew up, a bit west of the coast, and none of us kept much connection to Pollocksville. So I am unsettled as the miles go by, time slowing as I pass through a pine-framed territory that is at once distant and familiar. Through the changes of the present—the new houses, cleared land, new-built highways—comes the tug of the past, the glimpse of some house I saw as a child, some ruined storefront with a sign I remember, some curve of the road where a field stretched out, some churchyard or tree-lined street. I am a time traveler, moving into the past.

My first destination is New Bern, where the reunion banquet will be held on the second night; even forty years along, there are no hotels in Jones County where those of us coming from out of town can stay. My route carries me past Goldsboro, where my mother lives, and Kinston, another prominent eastern North Carolina town; both were once important tobacco markets, and Goldsboro was named a "Most Liveable City" in the country by *Money* magazine sometime back.

In Goldsboro, as I have learned, John Richards was lynched in 1916, accused but never convicted of the murder of a white man, the deed carried out by a mob of hundreds, the man castrated, tortured, shot. Goldsboro nowadays has the quiet feeling of a town in which a breeze barely stirs. I am picturing hundreds of white people, angry, hungry for the blood of a black man to the point that they break him out of jail, savagely kill him, mutilate his body, and commemorate the event in pictures. I have cousins, aunts, uncles, grandparents, who lived and died a few miles down the road. No doubt I had ancestors in the crowd that lynched Mr. Richards.

Or perhaps they were involved in the killing of Joseph Black, father of a young man accused of rape, who was murdered when the mob, hundreds of white people, failed to find the son and, so, turned on the father. Mr. Black was first attacked by that mob while in jail in Goldsboro, but, still in custody, was transported to Kinston, where he was finally killed by scores of men who broke into the jail. Kinston is twenty miles or so from

Goldsboro, a pleasant drive if one keeps the air conditioner working. In 1916, all along this route, people like me had called for the immediate killing, without trial, of the father of a man merely thought to have committed a crime. People like me had worked themselves into a frenzy of bloodlust, had demanded the death of a black man without recourse to the law. People I might have known, with whom I might have gone to a movie, or to a Wednesday prayer meeting, or to the pool hall, had transformed into a mob.

The world lit by this fierce afternoon sun hardly admits of such a possibility, the moving landscape contrasting with the relative stillness of the lanes of traffic, my hands gripping the steering wheel a bit too tight. The world has always been placid like this moment, settled into fields, roads, rivers, and towns, orderly patterns in which hardly anything moves. A few cattle stand near a watering hole. Horses lash their tails in a paddock within sight of the road. The land has such a dingy, settled look it would seem that scarcely anything out of the ordinary could ever have happened here, a deceptive sheen.

My route carries me along the border between Jones and Craven Counties, into New Bern, my destination for this trip. In New Bern, following the robbery of a store in 1905, a mob set on a man named John Moore, who was likely not the man they had chased out of the store but rather someone who was at hand when the chase went on too long. Mr. Moore was killed by the mob. His skin was black, like the skin of the man the mob had been chasing, and that was reason enough to kill him.

In Jones County, where I had lived for so long, Sheriff O. R. Colgrove and a companion, Amos Jones, were lynched during the Reconstruction era; Sheriff Colgrove was white, Mr. Jones was black. The sheriff, who might have been a carpetbagger, had been hindering Klan activities in the area, and so the Klan announced his murder, to be followed by a fine barbecue.

New Bern has become a thriving town, gorgeously sited at the conjunction of two rivers, taking advantage of its waterfront with hotels and a marina. Nearly all the stores along its main street are different from the ones I remember, which is hardly any surprise, since I've spent so little time here in the last decades. I used to chase my mother up and down these sidewalks when we came to town to shop for school clothes; Market Street still housed a couple of dime stores in those days, though even then there were larger stores at the edge of town. Now the street is home to health-food restaurants, coffee shops, and art galleries.

As I cruise through town, find my hotel and park, I am noticing the mingling of black and white people on the street, in the businesses, in the hotel as I register for my room. Public accommodations have not been segregated here for forty years or more, and no one pays any attention to the fact that blacks and whites move together in and out of shops, passing each other without much more than the occasional smile or nod of acknowledgment. In my earliest childhood, even the idea of such commonplace mingling of the races was looked on as a sign of doomsday, or of communism, or both. Here in New Bern, a town I knew pretty well in those days, I am seeing integration as if it just happened, as if my eyes are new.

I settle into the hotel room, check with the front desk to find out whether Mercy has arrived yet, and wonder whether I will recognize anyone at the church service to honor classmates who have already died. I thumb through the yearbook, faces and names from long ago, memories pushing forward.

THE HOTEL IS pleasant but ordinary, smelling of too much carpet cleaner, walls of glass facing the riverfront, friendly faces at the front desk, a basket of free cookies on the counter. I meet Mercy in the lobby and we chat a bit, catching up. We have been out of touch for a decade or more, but she is the same steady, sane voice I remember from high school, and any feeling of separation quickly disappears. We remained close friends through college in Chapel Hill, living together in the same house for most of a year. We finished our last college exam in the same class on the same morning. When I moved to New Orleans, I sold her my old car. She is one of the few people from Jones County with whom I have stayed in touch in any kind of consistent way.

We drive to Pollocksville for the memorial service, chattering about the last few years, other mutual friends, her son and husband. Like me, she's worried that she won't recognize anyone at the memorial service. We both wonder whether any white class-mates will show up. Years before, she and I attended what was supposed to be our tenth high school reunion, held at Quaker Neck Country Club, between Pollocksville and Trenton. As we learned when we arrived, that reunion was for the white stu-dents in our class, and included several people who had left the public schools as soon as integration was enforced. I never heard about a twenty-year reunion; for the thirtieth, there was a concerted effort to hold a true reunion of all the class, but I was traveling when that one was held.

At about dusk we cruise along the main street of Pollocks-ville. I am pierced with memories. The place appears unchanged except in cosmetic ways: a good deal of growth around the houses has been trimmed back or cleared, and thus many old houses are now visible near the river, buildings that were mostly hidden when I lived here. The boat landing is visible from the street, and the railroad depot that sat next to my house has been moved there and renovated. The village has the aura of a bedroom community in the making, though it shows its age, too, in the look of the houses. There is no Starbucks, no fast food, no strip mall; there is still little or no retail; some of the gas stations have closed; but the core of the place is the same as I remember. The single traffic light on Main Street, knocked down by truck a few years after I left for college, never was replaced. To travelers along Highway 17 the tiny hamlet must seem little more than a nuisance with a lower speed limit, the proverbial bump in the road.

The place looks so tiny now. Whereas earlier it was vast, my whole world.

The old Alex H. White Elementary School has been torn down, and a new school called Pollocksville Elementary School has taken its place on the same site. The J. W. Willie School is gone, too; so, in fact, even those traces of the dual school system have been erased. The practice of a prominent doctor has grown to fill most of an old field outside town. Some of the older houses have finally fallen into heaps, including the one that the actual Alex H. White built for his family on Main Street.

At the church I meet old friends, recognize them, we embrace, the awkwardness altogether endurable. As old people do, we tell each other how good we're looking, the phrase like a chant that crosses the crowd. It's a hot afternoon and I'm sweating in my jacket. No one else is wearing a tie, so I take mine off and put it in my pocket. When I was growing up here, no one would have contemplated walking into a church service without a tie.

During the service I gaze from face to face, seeing the contours of the younger self in the softening and aging of the older, face after face, person after person, leading me back through decades, seeing that courtyard between the wings of classrooms in our old high school, these bodies lounging against the cinderblock wall, fierce and restive where we are now easy and settled. The evening is full of talk of God and church and faith; I do not remember so much religious conversation in our high school days.

One person stands to give a eulogy for classmates who have died. Cousins speak for cousins; everyone in the county is second or third cousin to everyone else. What surprises me is that we are all so old, so full of gravitas; we look now so much like the adults who surrounded me when I was a child.

These are the people who stayed. A few of us have traveled here from other states, a few more from other towns, but many of these people have lived in Jones County all these years. Just as our teachers used to warn us, some of us would stay but most of us would leave, and many would never come back. Mercy and I are the only white classmates who showed up. At first I am aware of the absence of so many others; then, after a few minutes, I am simply in the room with people who mattered to me very much, whether I understood it then or not, once upon a time.

AFTER THE MEMORIAL service Mercy and I drive to Maysville for what is called, in the reunion schedule, a meet and greet. By now, after dark, I find that I can picture every bend in the road. In daylight, I might have seen differences, but in the dark it is as if I am riding down this road on a night long ago. We are riding through old plantation country; down Highway 17 in one direction lie the Foscue house and lands, still owned by members of the family; and in the other direction is Ravenwood, once a very large plantation owned by the Pollock family, whose ancestor gave the town its name. Just up the road from Hatchville is the old Oakview Farm and house, now called the Bell Farm, named for the family that has owned it for many decades. More plantations are mentioned in various historical records, owned by the McDaniel, Foy, Banks, Noble, and Whitaker families, to name a few. The 1850 census recorded 2,139 whites, 2,757 black slaves, and 142 free blacks living in Jones County, which was, at the time, a very wealthy place, if one defines wealth as what was owned by white people. The county would fall into poverty with the freeing of its wealth, which is to say the freeing of the slaves; nearly every narrative concerning the fortune of one of those old planter families includes the number of slaves it owned and how that number grew over time, this statistic outranking even the count of acres under cultivation.

How much of this land was cleared by the labor of slaves? By the forced labor of the ancestors of people I know, with whom I went to school? Some of these fields have been under cultivation since those days; in places, the outline of forest and field has hardly shifted since records have been kept. How many slaves were beaten, how many families separated and sold? What did white people do to enforce the subordination of black labor after the war? How far did we go to prove to ourselves that we were the superior ones? I know the general outlines of the answer; I know that the last person lynched in Jones County, Jerome Whitfield, was killed here in 1921, accused of the rape of a white woman. I can remember the days of separate bathrooms, water fountains, restaurants; I can remember black people deferring to my father as "Captain Jack," when they had no reason to respect him that I could see. I know that crosses were burned, I know that gangs of men roamed the night in trucks and cars, liquored up and ready for a fight. In the days of slavery they were slave patrollers, looking for runaways, stopping travelers on the road, checking to make sure no black person traveled without the proper paperwork. In the days of Reconstruction they were night riders, their purpose to perform acts of terror in the countryside. In the modern day they are good old boys, doing what good old boys have always done. In each age a different reason for the same pattern, white men policing the night.

How close did I come to being one of those men? To setting a lit match to the foot of a fuel-soaked cross?

The meet and greet is held at a small restaurant on the outskirts of Maysville, and we park in the crowded lot beside a neatly mowed ditch. The sky threatens rain as we head into the building. I have brought along a copy of the high school yearbook. Once inside, we eat fried chicken wings, raw vegetables and dip, cheese on a platter, while the yearbook passes from hand to hand. People are pointing to old pictures of themselves, hooting at the clothes, the hairdos. The room is cramped, the tables close together, so that we can shout from table to table. We trade stories about one another, about classmates who are not here, catch one another up on the last four decades. The talk is about boyfriends and girlfriends, football or basketball games, classes, rivalries, old stories of arguments with parents; no one mentions integration, the walkouts, the anger, the confrontations. We talk about the ordinary side of high school, dialogue that might be lifted from any number of generic class reunions as depicted on TV shows. There is something so very Jones County about this moment, all of us shoved into a room that is too small, chairs too close together, people climbing over each other to get to the food.

Here we are, nearly sixty years old, each of us fat and tired, heaving ourselves in and out of chairs with huffs and puffs, exactly as our parents and teachers used to do. I talk to Steven and his wife; I talk to Clarence Winkle, Andrew, Mercy, Barbara; the longer I'm in the room with these old friends and acquaintances, the more I recognize the younger faces within the old. It is fine that we talk about our high school days as if they were ordinary, simply a matter of remembering who dated whom; we all know better. The party ends early, when the chicken wings are eaten, and we drive home in the heavy rain that has begun to fall.

GOOD PEOPLE TAUGHT and still teach racism to their children without a second thought. This was true in the South of my birth and remains so to the present. Good people who would help a neighbor, including a black neighbor; people who would pray for the benefit of God's love; people who would never harm one of their own. We teach that like wants to be with like, and that this is only natural. We teach that white people should be allowed to have white schools, white churches, white social clubs, just like any other group. We teach that God created the races to be separate from one another for a purpose, and we preach that this purpose cannot be to mix, because why then would He have created the separation in the first place? We teach that when people are different from each other, one is better and the other worse.

We teach that black and white are not simply different but opposite. We reserve our special ideological fury for blackness.

What we avoid teaching and telling is what we did in the name of that difference once upon a time, in these fields and in these woods of eastern North Carolina. A superior race has the right to treat an inferior race as it chooses, including the right to reduce it to the status of property, to trade people like livestock, useful only for the labor that can be flogged out of them. This was the assumption our Southern culture embodied from the beginning. The history is there for anyone who chooses to learn it. But we refuse to face what that made of us, the whip hand that we became.

It is easy to see racism in the violent events, in lynchings and beatings, in rapes and other acts of terror. It is easy, too, to pretend that we are not racist if we did not take part in such overt acts. But I was taught to believe in white superiority in small ways, by gentle people, who believed themselves to be sharing God's own truth.

THE FOLLOWING NIGHT, at the banquet in the New Bern hotel, our class shares a meal, attends to presentations, and listens to Mrs. Corbin speak. She is nearing eighty, but healthy and strong-voiced, reminding us that our class made history, that we are part of the group that ended segregation, that we were a part of something important in the world. She refers briefly to the walkouts, reminding us that the problems in our high school had come from friction between the students and the administration, that we had played our part well, behaved well, and accomplished the change with grace. I am glad she spoke so directly.

I am the only white person from our class in the room tonight. Surely some of our white classmates could have come? Surely they heard about the event, since so many of them still live in the area?

Evelyn Hall comes to the banquet with her husband; other friends are present who were not with us the night before. For a few minutes I sit hand in hand with Ursula, and we talk about sixth grade, about our kiss, about the march from the high school to the school superintendant's office, about a play we did together in drama class, about a score of other moments we remember. Speaking in a rush, one as delighted as the other,

we run through the forty years we have been separated. She has
the same kind face, the same warm smile. We talk about Stella,
Mercy, Reginald, Barbara, Gary, others. She tells me Rhonda is
in Paris with her daughter, and I am struck by the wonder of it,
little country Rhonda now with a grown daughter, Rhonda an
established grownup visiting Europe.

We have all grown up, become more substantial, planted
ourselves here and there. Many of the men and women in the
room have spent years in the military. Many work as teachers.
Dreams have come true for some. The room sounds lively and
happy, and people are turning over the pages of the yearbook
again, reliving old rivalries, reminding each other that we were
once young together, faces turned outward from that old high
school, looking forward.

The dinner speaker, a local reverend, begins to deliver a sermon drawn from the New Testament parable about the prodigal son. He is making the point that a person gains significance
by helping others, and in some way this leads him to the tale of
the son who asks for his inheritance while his father is still alive.

Relaxed in my seat, I suddenly hear the minister say, "And
Mr. Grimsley, let me tell you. No black man would ever ask
his daddy to give him his inheritance early." The room erupts
in laughter, and I blush a bit and smile and make a show of
enjoying the joke.

A moment later, finishing the story, the minister refers to the
prodigal son as "the Jew-boy," and I shake my head in disbelief.

I lose the thread of what he is saying in contemplation of the epithet.

Am I really welcome here? Or would the rest of my classmates be happier if I had not come?

How many times in sixth grade did Rhonda and Ursula feel like this, alone in a crowd of white people who ranged from openly hostile to mildly friendly? The moment is a reminder that even these people, classmates from a troubled era, have their own flaws, their own biases, their own ideas of difference. We have a long way to go before we are ready to live together without the consciousness of race.

Later, as I am leaving, Clarence asks me if I have any idea why none of the other white classmates are here. Since he was our class president, it is his job to organize the reunions, so he wonders what he should do. Are the white people having a separate reunion? But he knows the answer as well as I do, I expect. There is still the old stubbornness, the same refusal, whites holding on to the notion that is so deeply rooted in us, that the white race should not mix, beyond a certain point, with those of other colors. That much has never changed. And tonight I wonder whether many of the black people here don't feel more or less the same.

Somewhere in my memory, beneath all I've learned and experienced, there is still the little bigot I was meant to be. I can hope that I've changed; I can question my upbringing; I can examine my life for every nuance of bias and prejudice and racism; but even so I can never erase that earliest software, those assumptions that were part of my surroundings from my first breath. This is why, whenever a white person tells me he or she is not a racist, I never believe the statement. What we learn in those earliest months and years can never be deleted.

But this fact was never a doom or a destiny. I changed. I learned to question the programming. When Violet Strahan spoke back to me in sixth grade, after I decided to call her a black bitch, something crumbled in my vision of the world. In her response she was defiantly, loudly, brazenly human, and she blazed with the fact of herself. I had thought to call her a name and score points with the other white kids. I had thought that she would be meek because she was black. I had thought she agreed with me that I was superior to her. No one was more surprised than me to learn that I was wrong on all counts. She cracked open the invisibility barrier right away. She let me know how completely present she was.

This was no moment of revelation so much as simple recognition. I was too young for anything more abstract. She was like people I knew; when she was angry I could feel it; and when she spoke and looked me in the eye, I understood the power of her person. She was everything I had been told that black people were not. She was haughty and superior in her tone. She schooled me like a child. She was not the least bit hesitant.

For me this was the crucial moment. Maybe if this confrontation with Violet had failed to get through to me, I would still have learned this lesson at some other time. But I understood in an instant that there was no difference between Violet, Rhonda, Ursula, me, or any of the rest of us. This was not comprehension that was conscious, but was something deeper, a knowing from the bone. I had no need to articulate it; the feeling was true in my body.

When Ursula kissed me on the cheek in seventh grade, I felt flushed and warm. When Rhonda looked at pictures of Davy Jones with me, I felt accepted and safe. When Mr. Wexler listened to my opinions about Hubert Humphrey and Richard Nixon, I felt respected as an intellect. During the first dance at high school, I fell into the same rhythm as everybody else on the floor, joining them for a moment. As the protests unfolded later over those two winters, I felt exhilarated that people were acting out in my high school, speaking their minds, taking action as a group. What they did made us part of the world. Violet had knocked me open. A confrontation with the facts had knocked my head open. Everybody in my town and in my high school had that choice to make, whether to see each other as equals and move on in one direction, or else to refuse and move on in another. There were no other paths.

Now I am packing my suitcase in the hotel room, looking out the window over the parking lot at the distant line of roofs of downtown New Bern. There is still so much of me that feels a close connection to this place, the more so now because I am here and so much is familiar. I pack the car and head toward home, but this morning I travel the long way, down Highway 17 to Pollocksville, past Rhems Church, 10 Mile Fork Road, Green Valley, Killis Murphy Road, through the little village and up Highway 58 toward Trenton. The old high school sits halfway there, in the same field. I can see some new outbuildings, but the core of the school is just as it was when I stood in that courtyard, books under my arm, hearing the bell for class. I sit in my car for a while, parked by the side of the road, staring at the old bricks, at the flagpole, at the empty parking lot.

I can see us all standing in the smoking patio, staring over that field, vain and young and sure of ourselves. In my mind it is the month before high school is over, I am about to graduate, and my long life in Jones County is soon to end. My only thought is that I want to fly away. Now, so much later, I find I am still rooted here.

Maybe it is the fact of the reunion that sums it all up in my head. We were the mighty Trojans of the Class of 1973, the fourth graduating class of a new high school composed of all the students of the county. We slouched from class to class, adopted the poses of coolness, turned up our noses at one another in the cafeteria, called each other names, gossiped, spread stories false and true, speculated about who was with who, speculated about who was still a virgin, talked about politics in mostly uninformed ways. White people declared that the South would rise again. Black people raised one fist and chanted for Black Power. Somehow we negotiated a space between those poles and learned to sit in classrooms together. In some cases we made friendships. Some of us fell in love. The heavens neither trembled nor opened, nor did earthquakes crack the ground. God's wrath failed to show itself, and the mixing of the races, as it turned out, was simply one more change that we learned to accept, whether happily or grudgingly. We learned to live in the presence of one another. We were the ones who desegregated Jones County public schools, black and white, male and female, sullen and stormy, happy and giddy, wanton and drunken, cool and slouched, shy and lost. Lawyers, judges, adults declared that the days of separate schools were over, but we were the ones who took the next step. History gave us a piece of itself. We made of it what we could.

A Conversation with
Jim Grimsley and Anne Rasmussen

Reprinted with permission of "Late Night Library" and
"LateNightLibrary.org"

1. Almost fifty years have passed since that first school year, in 1966, when your sixth-grade classroom in rural Jones County, North Carolina admitted its first black pupils in response to the Freedom of Choice Act. And yet cultural tensions related to race are still very much a part of our current national conversation. You've obviously thought deeply and reflectively about these issues since the moment your own small-town, Southern, white world expanded to include those three black girls, and with them a discovery: that a world existed beyond what you had been taught to expect. What made you decide to write about this particular experience now, and why as a memoir rather than a novel (or play)?

The idea of the book came to me at least a couple of decades ago, and perhaps a bit more; I realized at some point that there had been rather little written about this event by white Southern writers. The idea for the book underwent a good deal of transformation as I considered it. My original idea was to write a memoir, but to mix fiction into it in order to make it both dramatic and true. I knew that a memoir would have a greater feeling of authority than a piece of fiction about this era, but I was constrained in making the attempt by the fact that I had already written a good deal of autobiographical fiction about this era of my life, and I did not want to write a repeat of that. My childhood story involved a number of powerful elements; I grew up in a family that was plagued by the violence of my father, his alcoholism, and the chronic illness, hemophilia, that my brother and I lived with. I told the story of this family in my first novel, *Winter Birds*, so I was aware of the power of the material. My fear was that these aspects of the story would cloud the focus of any memoir I might write about my early years.

I did a lot of reading over the last two decades to prepare me for this writing, and meanwhile pondered how best to shape the story. I read books about eastern North Carolina history, about the type of slavery that was practiced there, about the Civil War and reconstruction. I read slave narratives recorded during the Works Progress Administration (WPA) era, which were oral histories taken from slaves who had survived in Piedmont and eastern North Carolina. This reading taught me that I actually knew very little of my own history; the process showed me that while Southerners might be reputed to be great storytellers and sharers of their own history, the history that we had handed down to ourselves in Jones County was incomplete.

About six years ago I felt that it was time to take on this book and set out to write it. I chose to shape it as a novel, hoping that later I would be able to weave some chapters of memoir into the fictional narrative. In framing the novel I chose a child of a family different from my own, but I told his story using largely the facts of my sixth-grade class as I remembered them. That story encompassed only the sixth-grade year when Freedom of Choice was in play in North Carolina, the year that the three black girls came to our class. I finished a manuscript of the book that was some four hundred pages in length, showed it to my publisher and to some other people, and got lukewarm reactions to the story all around. Rejection was painful, as it always is, and it took me a few months to work through their responses and to understand that the failure was mine. My editor at Algonquin saw the book as promising and offered some very specific suggestions to make it better, but while I knew these were good ideas, I also knew they were not what I wanted to do.

I decided to write a manuscript in which I simply wrote down everything I could remember about my encounters with black people and with the idea of blackness, reaching back as far as I could go. When I started this work, I very quickly realized that I was writing material that was vastly stronger than the novel. My fears about the memoir proved unfounded, as I was able very easily to limit the writing to the subject of integration and to limit the material about my family. My story was largely that of my own transformation from a young bigot to something that I now term a recovering bigot, someone who still has racist programming but who refuses to act on it, much the way that an alcoholic recovers by refusing to drink one day at a time.

When I showed this manuscript to my editor, he became excited about the book, and he saw what I was trying to do with this story very clearly; he helped me to reshape that manuscript into the present book.

2. I'm interested in the point you make about growing up without knowing the true history of your own region in regards to race. (I think this could be said of white folks in other regions as well—the ability to remain ignorant of this history is a pretty major indicator of white privilege.) Can you give an example of a detail that you encountered in your research that particularly surprised you, either because it deviated sharply from your personal recollections or changed your own understanding of a memory from this time?

When I read the history of lynchings in eastern North Carolina, I was struck by the fact that the people who were involved in these events might have been friends and family. There's a whole brutal history to the way our country was settled, and I knew it in outline, but the impact of it did not come home to me until I read about the lynching of men in Wayne County, in Lenoir County, and in Jones County, where at least three men were killed by mob violence. I pictured my relatives, my acquaintances, my friends, even myself in these crowds, and the feeling was startling and unpleasant. The last man was hung in Jones County sometime in the 1930s, about the time my parents were born. Understanding that such acts had taken place in my home, where I thought of people as gentle and kindly, made me understand how much bigger the history was than I had realized.

3. One thing that really struck me about the first section of the book, which follows the first year that Violet, Ursula, and Rhonda join your class, is how overwhelmingly silent the adults in your world (parents, teachers, and other whites in your community) are on the subject of race relations or desegregation. The teacher introduces the new girls as though they'd simply moved there from another town. And you and your white classmates receive no real cues from adults about how you are expected to respond or behave in this unprecedented situation: you and your peers are left to decipher the silence. Whereas the three newcomers (not having the luxury to ignore—or pretend to ignore—their racial difference) seem quite a bit more prepared for the possibility of

confrontation. You and your sixth-grade classmates learn by trial and error what you can and can't say or do; you form friendships and alliances in spite of (or perhaps because of) this. What do you imagine caused such a total silence on the part of the adults in your world, particularly your teachers, in the face of this tremendous cultural shift?

I think the people in my little town felt a deep discomfort with the whole idea of race and that they kept silent about the process of integration for a whole spectrum of reasons. So when I say that the community was silent on the subject, what I mean is that there was no consensus, no open discussion, no preparation for integration. White Southerners were deeply conflicted about civil right legislation and about the end of the two separate school systems. Some whites openly opposed integration; some saw it as inevitable; some even approved of it but looked on its coming with trepidation, not certain what this enormous change would do to what we called our "way of life."

People kept silent about this issue because to pursue it too directly would bring about conflict, and the adults I knew did not like open discussions of anything controversial. It's not the way of small-town people to discuss their feelings, their problems, their fears. The idea of integration was very frightening to people and so they ignored it as much as they could. When somebody mentioned integration at our church, usually in a negative way, the subject hung in the air uncomfortably for a moment or two and then disappeared again. This is what I remember from the people I knew.

There were exceptions, I'm sure. There were parents who told their children to respect the black students in our classrooms, though I can remember only one or two families in which this kind of conversation took place, and I only learned about those families much later. In my own family, issues of survival overpowered even the idea of integration.

There had to have been some discussions about integration among the adults that went further than those to which I was exposed, because many white people took action to oppose the consolidation of schools. Private schools were formed in our county and the neighboring county, starting around 1968. I have no idea what this process was like, but it had to involve a good deal of discussion.

The silence of our schoolteachers on this subject was the most surprising to me. My elementary schoolteachers were nearly all women, very strong-minded people, and I doubt they would have been afraid of this kind of conversation without good reason. It's possible they felt they could not control such a discussion in their classroom; it's possible that some of them did not approve of integration or that they did not want to teach black students; it's possible that they did not want to come into conflict with our parents by having such discussions. I simply don't know why there was so little preparation for this process on the part of the schools.

4. In 1968 the Supreme Court rules Freedom of Choice insufficient to integrate the public schools, and a more enforced plan of busing and integration follows. Many of your white peers abandon the public system in favor of hastily created private schools, and you find yourself in the minority in high school, hoping to fit in with an entirely new set of peers. And there are institutional challenges as well: the teaching staff is mostly white and many are inexperienced new teachers working off their educational debt. Some resent having to teach black students and make racist remarks. When your black peers attempt to address these issues by staging a walkout, it's reframed as a "riot" in subsequent reports. You and your classmates forged alliances, friendships, and romances across racial boundaries within the self-contained world of the school. And yet outside of school, most folks reverted to their (separate) communities. You were the only white person to attend your fortieth high school reunion—one classmate even asked you if the whites were holding a separate reunion elsewhere. What do you think could have been done to make these connections more lasting and meaningful over time?

The personal connections that we made were in fact lasting and meaningful over time, at least to some of us. Facebook brought me back in touch with a lot of my high school friends, and the sense of connection we feel to one another is palpable. Living through those years was intense for all of us, and it forged bonds that are strong. The people I knew in high school can cut through to my core very easily and quickly, and some of them still do so, even in the shortest message on my Facebook page. I have a reverence for those folks that is not like any of my other friendships. They remind me of my childhood; they call me by my childhood name, Jimmy. They saw me at my worst and weakest, before I had developed my adult ability to disguise myself.

It's hard for me to speculate about why the white students did not come to the reunion because I don't live there any more. There are a lot of reasons that make it hard to face people you knew in high school; there is likely still to be a reluctance on the part of blacks and whites to socialize with one another, especially in groups. Since writing the book I have heard that the practice of holding racially segregated reunions is not all that uncommon in the South even today, and I expect this reflects a continued reluctance on the part of white people to accept integration at the social level. White people by and large do not see black people as their social equals, and this is particularly true in rural areas.

However, I know from talking to some of my friends in Jones County that the line of separation between the races is far easier to cross than it was fifty years ago. There has been a lot of intermarriage in the intervening decades, and most families are now integrated to some degree. It is easier now for white people and black people to maintain friendships and to visit one another in their homes. The world changes in part and stays the same in part.

I think our biggest failure during those early years of integration was to fail at organized dialog with one another, and I fault the adults in Jones County for this. There were no active parent groups who stepped forward to encourage black and white students to talk to one another about the process of integration. It would have made a big difference if we had learned to discuss how it felt to be part of this enormous change. But those kinds of guided conversations were not all that common in any arena in the 1960s and 70s. Counseling was much less visible and active in that time.

5. In the middle section of the book, "ORIGINS," you explore the ways in which bigoted ideas of race first entered your consciousness, possibly as early as you learned to speak. The word "nigger" enters your lexicon through nursery rhymes and children's songs, in overheard jokes and stories, and in its casual, widespread usage as an adjective for "substandard." Though you are taught not to use the word in conversation (it was "coarse"), its negative meaning and association with black people was clear. And in church, (your mother's claim to cultural respectability) the symbolism is underscored: white is equated to goodness and black to evil and sin. You have this rooted notion of social order related

to skin color long before you enter school, much less encounter any black people. I loved the detail and sensitivity with which you unpack these early childhood experiences. (I was reminded of the playwright Adrienne Kennedy's examination of her own earliest impressions of race—like her fascination with Snow White—in her memoir, *People Who Led to My Plays*.) Since many of these early impressions were subconsciously formed, at what point did you become explicitly aware of them as bigoted?

I only examined the process that taught me racist ideas about blackness and black people when I was writing these chapters. I remember approaching the writing of these chapters with a good deal of anxiety, since I was not sure I would be able to find the earliest bits of this programming in myself. But once I started to write, I saw more and more deeply into what I had learned as a very young child. The chapter about the nursery rhymes was one of the first pieces of the book that I wrote, and I remember being horrified as I was writing those rhymes in which the word "nigger" appeared as a kind of chant. We spoke these lines of doggerel in play, but play is a very important part of shaping a child's world.

I only became aware of myself as a racist when I encountered the girls in my sixth-grade class, and even then my awareness was not very deep. By the time I was in high school I was able to discuss bias-issues with what passes for clarity among teenagers, but I had no real understanding of how pervasive an issue it was in our county. In college I became aware of black political movements, and my own coming out as a gay person began to educate me in the mechanics of oppression. After college I moved to New Orleans, where the problems between whites and blacks were visible everywhere; and after I moved to Atlanta I worked for twenty years in the public hospital here, Grady Memorial, where the patient population is largely black and where the staff is largely black. So throughout my life I have worked and lived in settings that were far from homogenous or white. This taught me a great deal about the way white people maintain power even in settings where black people predominate, but once again these were lessons that only became explicit to me when I started to write about them.

6. How did those early lessons in language, storytelling, and symbolism shape your sensibilities as a writer?

These ideas are still shaping me as a writer. In my early years I was reluctant to write black characters into my work because I did not want to be seen as attempting to speak on behalf of black people. Those first books were mostly about the lives of poor white people, the class from which I emerged, and my focus there was on working through material related to my family. The first story I wrote in which I dealt with race overtly was a story called, "Jesus is Sending You This Message," the tale of a fussy, uncomfortable white bachelor who tells a black preacher woman to shut up on a commuter train in Atlanta. Her bold willingness to preach in public frightens him and makes him afraid that his own Christianity is tepid. After writing that story I began to be more bold about writing overtly on subjects of race. The novel I am currently working on tells the story of the transfer of administrative power from white people to black people at Grady Memorial Hospital, a process that I witnessed while I was there.

* * *

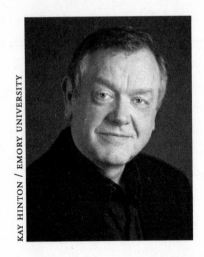

Jim Grimsley is the author of several award-winning novels, including *Winter Birds*, *Dream Boy*, and *My Drowning*. He is a professor at Emory University.